110592

evelyn waugh

88

The Christian Critic Series

evelyn waugh

Edited by
ROBERT MURRAY DAVIS

Contributors

D. J. DOOLEY
ALVIN B. KERNAN
BERNARD BERGONZI
CHARLES E. LINCK, JR.
ROBERT MURRAY DAVIS
MARSTON LaFRANCE
PATRICIA CORR

B. HERDER BOOK CO.
314 NORTH JEFFERSON
ST. LOUIS, MISSOURI 63103

The Christian Critic Series is under the general editorship of Harry J. Cargas, Director of the Foreign Student Program, Saint Louis University.

Library of Congress Catalog Card No. 72-79293

In Memoriam

R. J. MURRAY (1885-1957)

ELIZABETH MURRAY DAVIS (1909-1966)

INTRODUCTION

Two years after his death and forty years after the publication of his first novel, Evelyn Waugh seems to be one of the few English novelists of the 1930's whose work is likely to prove of enduring interest and value. His novels continue to attract a wide and appreciative audience, not only among critics but among graduate and undergraduate students of all shades of political and religious opinion. He is not, in quite the same sense of Graham Greene or in any thing like the dreary sense of Catholic reviewers of the late forties, primarily a "Catholic novelist." As J. F. Powers once stated matters: "It would be silly for Catholics to look to him for the kind of books already written by Bernanos and Greene and others. He does not seem to have the heart for that, nor, what is more discernible, the desire. I for one am not sorry about that." [1] Essentially, Waugh is a satirist, though he once denied it, [2] and in his best work he gives his readers not only marvellously funny and technically accomplished novels but a vision of modern chaos which anyone can recognize and a criticism of it to which anyone can assent—anyone, that is, who is capable of understanding and appreciating satire. [3]

Much of the best critical work has concentrated on Waugh as satirist rather than as Catholic. This is understandable, since Waugh's most successful work is generally, though by no means universally, acknowledged by Catholic and non-Catholic alike to be the satiric novels of the thirties. Some of the critics in this volume deal not with the theological dimension of Waugh's novels but rather with their portrayal of the secular human scene—what Waugh himself called "the world of wild aberration without theological significance." [4] These critics are far from indifferent to values—Kernan, for example, is aware of

Waugh's relationship to traditional religious and political tenets—but they see the values as embodied in the novels, as given in works of art, rather than seeking to argue with them or to promulgate them.

Other critics, more tendentious, have gone so far as to insist that Waugh is not, as far as his imagination is concerned, really Catholic at all, though some see this as grounds for condemnation, others for congratulation. Ironically, much of the condemnation has fallen upon *Brideshead Revisited,* the most overtly Catholic (save *Helena,* which is part novel, part hagiography) of Waugh's novels. Donat O'Donnell and others hold that the central subject of *Brideshead* is not, as Waugh put it, "the operation of divine grace on a group of diverse but closely connected characters," [5] but something like a romantic, or a snobbish, or a sentimental, or simply a distorted picture of the aristocracy and its enemies. [6] The congratulations on Waugh's non-Catholic imagination have come from both Catholic and secular critics, and these encomiums are frequently used to extol the early work and condemn later novels which have overtly Catholic subjects like *Brideshead* and *Sword of Honour,* the one-volume version of Waugh's war trilogy. These critics argue that Waugh buried or misused his talent by taking positive stands on political and religious matters. As Sean O'Faolain puts it,

Being a man of genius, he should never, under any circumstances, have opinions, for whenever he has written out of his opinions it becomes all too plain over again that imagination is a soaring gull and opinions no more than a gaggle of ungainly starlings, chattering angrily in a cornfield. Opinions breed anger, nourish hate, ossify the heart, narrow the mind. [7]

One might observe that satirists have never been noted for their tolerance, though it is true that they work best by indirection. After the war, one must admit, Waugh's public pronouncements tended to be crotchety or consciously provoking, and although remarkably little of this curmudgeonliness was carried into the novels, even a little is enough to seriously if not fatally mar the tone of a book. Some of the adverse criticism of Waugh's novels seems to be motivated by partisan religious or political irritation. Such criticism is irrelevant—as, for that matter, is merely partisan praise.

However, not all of the strictures against the later work can be thus easily dismissed, for many of them are based upon arguments that the later works—notably *Brideshead,* which has been occasion and focus of discussions of Waugh's later manner—is artistically flawed. Waugh himself seemed to admit as much, for he revised *Brideshead* and denounced its style and temper as severely as any hostile critic [8] and even characterized as "sentimental delusion" the mood in which he wrote it. [9] Moreover, he did not include three late novels, *Scott-King's Modern Europe* (1947), *Helena* (1950), and *The Ordeal of Gilbert Pinfold* (1957), in the new collected edition published by Chapman and Hall between 1960 and 1967. Of the early fiction, only *Work Suspended,* a fragment, and the short story collection *Mr. Loveday's Little Outing* were thus treated.

Although estimates of the comparative and intrinsic merit of Waugh's novels have tended to agree, the final word has obviously not been said about them. For one thing, it is clear that no evaluation will be complete without a careful consideration of his religious attitudes. At present, not enough is known about them. The time is past when it is possible to assume that a shared Catholic faith enables anyone to speak with authority about such matters, but while mere demurrers or generalized defenses are at best superfluous, informed discussion can prove invaluable. Moreover, the perspective of time may alter the evaluation of Waugh's social and religious attitudes and of their expression in the later novels, for even more than most authors, a satirist can be seen objectively and evaluated dispassionately only after the causes and institutions he has assaulted and championed have passed into history. [10] In the meantime, we have a number of illuminating if not definitive discussions of the novels. Far more important, Waugh's undeniable achievement in those novels remains to be understood and enjoyed.

ROBERT MURRAY DAVIS

NOTES

1 J. F. Powers "Waugh Out West," *Commonweal,* XLVIII (July 16, 1948), 327.

2 Evelyn Waugh, "Fan-Fare," *Life,* XX (April 8, 1946), 60.

3 Many readers are not. See Frederick J. Stopp's account of *The Tablet's* condemnation of *Black Mischief* in *Evelyn Waugh: Portrait of an Artist* (Boston: Little, Brown, and Co., 1958), pp. 31-34. A subjective recent view is given in Gabriel Fielding's "Evelyn Waugh: The Price of Satire," in *Listener,* LXXII (1964), 541-542.

4 Evelyn Waugh, *Monsignor Ronald Knox* (Boston: Little, Brown, and Co., 1959), p. 314.

5 Evelyn Waugh, "Preface," *Brideshead Revisited* (revised edition; London: Chapman and Hall, 1960), p. 9.

6 Representative of this type of criticism is Donat O'Donnell (Conor Cruise O'Brien), *Maria Cross: Imaginative Patterns in a Group of Modern Catholic Writers* (Toronto: Oxford University Press, 1952), pp. 119-134. Paul A. Doyle summarizes the attacks on Waugh's Catholicism by Catholics and non-Catholics in "The Persecution of Evelyn Waugh," in *America,* XCIX (May 3, 1958), 165, 168-169.

7 Sean O'Faolain, *The Vanishing Hero* (Boston: Little, Brown and Co., 1957), p. 43.

8 See his "Preface" to the revised edition.

9 Evelyn Waugh, *A Little Learning* (Boston: Little, Brown and Co., 1964), p. 191.

10 Even now the disclosures of the Philby spy case in England are putting into a new perspective Waugh's accusations of Communist conspiracy in *Sword of Honour.* What had seemed a disgruntled Tory version of McCarthyism is now shown to have some basis in fact.

Contents

Contents

Alvin B. Kernan

THE WALL AND THE JUNGLE:
THE EARLY NOVELS OF EVELYN WAUGH

In Evelyn Waugh's novel *Helena*, Constantius, father of
the future Roman emperor Constantine, rides with his
bride Helena, later St. Helena the discoverer of the true
cross, along the rough Roman wall which separates Gaul
from Germany, forming the outermost defense of the City
of Rome. He explains to Helena the meaning of the wall:

Think of it, mile upon mile, from snow to desert, a single
great girdle round the civilized world; inside, peace, decency,
the law, the altars of the Gods, industry, the arts, order; outside, wild beasts and savages, forest and swamp, bloody mumbo-jumbo, men like wolf-packs; and along the wall the armed
might of the Empire, sleepless, holding the line. Doesn't it
make you see what the City means?

On one side of a guarded wall, barbarism, on the other,
civilization; on one side animals, on the other social man;
on one side the jungle, on the other The City; on one side
chaos, on the other order. This speech renders in geo-
graphical terms a master image of life which underlies
most of Waugh's novels. In his hard-headed, classical view
of life the powers which threaten civilization are ineradic-
able, and the opposing forces are distinctly separated, barbarism and chaos on the outside, civilization and order on
the inside, with the ceaselessly manned wall in between.
But in the postwar England of the '20's and '30's, the

From *Yale Review*, LIII (1963/64), 199-220. Copyright Yale
University. Reprinted by permission of the publisher.

basic scene of Waugh's first four satiric novels—*Decline and Fall* (1928), *Vile Bodies* (1930), *Black Mischief* (1932), and *A Handful of Dust* (1934)—the walls have already been broached and the jungle powers were at work within The City.

Decline and Fall, his first novel, opens with a night brawl in the quadrangle of Scone College, Oxford. High up in the walls of the College sit the remaining defenders of order, education, and tradition—the Junior Dean, Mr. Sniggs, and the Domestic Bursar, Mr. Postlethwaite. Their lights are extinguished so that they will not be seen by the rioting members of the Bollinger Club holding their annual meeting. From below in the darkness comes the shrill sound of the "English county families baying for broken glass," and out into the quad dressed in bottle-green evening coats rush the members of the Boller, "epileptic royalty from their villas of exile; uncouth peers from crumbling country seats; smooth young men of uncertain tastes from embassies and legations; illiterate lairds from wet granite hovels in the Highlands; ambitious young barristers and Conservative candidates torn from the London season and the indelicate advances of debutantes." Savagely drunk, they break up a grand piano, smash a china collection, throw a Matisse into a waterjug, have "great fun" with the manscript of a Newdigate Prize Poem found in an undergraduate's room, and round off their evening by debagging and throwing into a fountain a passing student whose school tie happens to resemble that of the Bollinger Club. Above, the two dons creep to the window, peer out, and anticipate huge fines, which will provide a week of Founder's port for the senior common room. The Junior Dean, hoping for even larger fines, prays, "Oh, please God, make them attack the Chapel," but unfortunately the members of the Boller begin to get sick and pass out. Next day authority reasserts itself with all its pomp and ceremony: in solemn assembly the officers of Scone fine the undergraduate members of the Bollinger Club, insuring Founder's port for the high table, and send down the young man who was debagged for indecent behavior with the awesome words, "That sort of young man does the College no good."

Nearly every scene in Waugh's satiric novels is built on the pattern of the Scone College scene. When an actual wall appears, its form and history betray its inability to hold out the forces of barbarism. The machiolated, towered, and turreted wall—with workable portcullis—around Llanabba Castle in *Decline and Fall* was built by unemployed mill workers during the cotton famine of the 1860's. The ladies of the house were upset by the thought of the men starving and went so far as to hold a charity bazaar to raise money for relief; the husband, a Lancashire millowner influenced by the Liberal economics, was equally upset by the thought of giving the men money "without due return." Sentimentality and enlightened self-interest were both neatly satisfied by putting the men to work on the wall. "A great deal of work was done very cheaply," and the Victorian taste for the romantic was satisfied by the neo-Gothic character of the construction which transformed plain Llanabba House into Llanabba Castle. The shabby, self-satisfied, and self-glorifying attitudes which caused the wall to be built were merely degraded remnants of older, more meaningful beliefs in such values as work and responsibility toward one's workers and fellow men. Already well along the way toward barbarism themselves, these Victorian attitudes offer no real resistance to the forces of destruction, and the wall they built is overwhelmed in the next century when the house becomes a boys' school which shelters every kind of greed, ignorance, and savagery.

While actual stone walls are not always present in Waugh's scenes, the immaterial walls of culture are. The traditions, the social institutions, the ritual language, the buildings, the manners, the morals, the codes of service, the esthetic values, "all that seemingly solid, patiently built, gorgeously ornamented structure of Western Life," are for the classicist like Waugh the walls protecting sense, order, and meaningful life from riot and savagery. One of the major effects of Waugh's writing comes from the ceremonial fullness with which these values are voiced and acted out. Dignified judges speak with timeless authority of the right of society to repress ruthlessly those "human vampires who prey upon the degradation of their species"; earnest custom officials meticulously sift all incoming books to exclude any writings which might affect the moral welfare of the English people; His Britannic Majesty's ministers are sent to far-flung and savage lands to protect truth and justice and show the more unfortunate peoples of the earth the way to civilization; the children destined to rule the nation are sent to ancient public schools where their minds and characters are carefully formed; the inquiring mind presses forward to the discovery of new truths about man and his universe; and social gatherings are enriched with names evoking ancient glory and service, "the fifteenth Marquess of Vanburgh, Earl Vanburgh of Brendon, Lord of the Five Isles and Hereditary Grand Falconer to the Kingdom of Connaught."

All this is, of course, a magnificent, hilarious sham. The judge who defends society with such sonorous certainty is condemning an innocent, powerless man and letting the real criminal go free. The earnest custom officials ferret out and burn Dante with the solemn warning that "if we can't stamp out literature in this country, we can at least stop its being brought in from the outside." The Envoy Extraordinary to Azania has forgotten how to speak all foreign languages, even French, and spends his time in the legation bathtub playing with rubber animals. A new master at a public school who asks what he should try to teach the boys is handed a heavy stick and told, "Oh, I shouldn't try to *teach* anything, not just yet, anyway. Just keep them quiet." Scientific inquiry continues its onward march with such inventions as the Huxdane-Hallay bomb, "for the dissemination of leprosy germs," and the spirit of Mill and Darwin descends to the sociologist Sir Wilfred Lucas-Dockery, the warden of Blackstone Gaol, who theorizes that men become criminals because of thwarted creative instincts: putting his theory to practice he provides a mad prisoner with a set of carpenter's tools, which the victim of thwarted creative instincts at once uses to cut off the Chaplain's head. The Hereditary Grand Falconer to the Kingdom of Connaught turns out to be a gossip columnist for *The Daily Beast*.

Waugh has frequently been accused of being a snob and deadly conservative, but in fact he treats the representatives of the old order as savagely as he does the new barbarians. He defends tradition, not the *status quo;* social order, not the establishment. The standards against which his fools are measured and found to be fools is not, in his early novels, located in any individual but in the values and social forms to which his characters without knowing what they are doing still give voice. Waugh is ultimately, like the chief character of *Brideshead Revisited,* a painter of old houses, an architectural painter who arrives to fix in paint the stately old houses of England just before the auctioneer and the demolition crew go to work to make room for shops and modern two-room apartments. And like Charles Ryder, Waugh finds his ultimate values in building, "holding it to be not only the highest achievement of man but one in which, at the moment of consummation, things were most clearly taken out of his hands and perfected, without his intention, by other means." Individual men, on the other hand, are less important, "something much less than the buildings they made and inhabited . . . mere lodgers, and short-term lessees of small importance in the long, fruitful life of their homes."

In Waugh's England there is no possibility of eradicating the powers of savagery and dullness which are destroying the old houses and social traditions they symbolize, for the powers are rooted in life itself; and by their very nature they continue to press against the walls and creep between the building stones of old houses as persistently as the lush vegetation of jungle—to which they are frequently compared—edges in to tear apart the building stones and choke the streets of abandoned cities. The most fundamental of these powers is a deeply ingrained, apparently indestructible tendency in man himself toward disorder, anarchy, and violence — toward those tendencies which Pope summed up as dullness. At times these dark powers appear undisguised in cannibal feast, jungle dances, savage riots and battlefields. But even in the great cities of the West the sounds of this ancient anarchy are always in the background, like the jungle drums which always beat in the hills just outside the city of Debra Dowa where the Emperor Seth in *Black Mischief* attempts to create a modern state. It appears, only slightly disguised, as the insane and murderous carpenter. It is the epileptic royalty, savage lairds, and ruthless politicians of the Bollinger Club. Or it may take shape as the random sexuality of Brenda Last or the charming ruthlessness of a "howling cad" like Basil Seal, the brutality of a Colonel MacAdder or a General Strapper, the deviations of Miles Malpratice and Mrs. Panrast, and the far-flung operations of the Latin American Entertainment Company, Ltd., Lady Metroland's efficient chain of South American brothels. Nature is seldom more beneficent than man, and the detructive powers in humanity have their natural correspondents in the nervous horse which kicks to death a small boy on his first hunt, the battering sea which the travelers cross at the opening of *Vile Bodies,* and the malarial mosquito which destroys Tony Last's chance of escape from the jungles of Brazil in *Handful of Dust.* Waugh's world is, in short, one in which life and order are threatened constantly from within and without.

No one who lives in this world takes it for anything other than familiar, secure Old England. But the pretenses are stripped away, unknowingly of course, by the Christmas sermon of an addled minister who somehow forgets that he is no longer the chaplain of a regiment on foreign service:

How difficult it is for us . . . to realize that this is Christmas. Instead of the glowing log fire and windows tight shuttered against the drifting snow, we have only the harsh glare of an alien sun; instead of the happy circle of loved faces, of home and family, we have the uncomprehending stares of the subjugate, though no doubt grateful, heathen. Instead of the placid ox and ass of Bethlehem . . . we have for companions the ravening tiger and the exotic camel, the furtive jackal and the ponderous elephant. . . .

The clergyman speaks with a peculiar kind of emptiness created by the absence of both heart and mind. The emptiness first appears in Waugh's novels as an extreme form of traditional English reticence, then expands to the point demanded by caricature; great voids are gradually opened up behind the foreheads and in the hearts of the dramatis personae. They have no private minds, no intense feelings whatsover; no personality, no individuality—whatever we call that reality of self which has been the subject of most of the writing of our age. As we encounter character after character of this kind, the world of the satiric novels slowly fills with automatons composed of ready-made, fashionable phrases. Their names tell us all there is to know about them: Lady Circumference and her son little Lord Tangent, the Earl of Pastmaster, Paul Pennyfeather, Lord Maltravers, the Minister of Transportation, Basil Seal, Agatha Runcible.

The use of type characters is, of course, common in satire, for the satirist is never interested in deep explorations of human nature. His characters are merely personifications of the particular form of dullness to which he wishes to give visible shape. But what in some satirists is an artistic device for getting dullness out into the open by disentangling it from the complexities of real character becomes in Waugh realism of sorts. He sings the rich, the powerful, the fashionable, and the fortunate; and he shows them to be as stiff, empty, and mechanical as fictive abstractions. On the rare occasions when there are hints that a character is feeling or thinking it comes as a great surprise to both character and reader. Who would have thought that the butterfly Agatha Runcible in *Vile Bodies* had any mind to lose? Or that Simon Balcairn, the aristocrat turned gossip columnist in the same novel, could have felt enough despair to make suicide necessary? Even when such actions establish a rudimentary mind or heart, the thought and emotions which emerge have a primitive, childlike quality, as if the owners were completely unused to such functions as thinking and feeling.

This all-pervasive simplicity and mindlessness is the principal cause of the trouble in Waugh's satiric world. What hope for the future when the full exercise of intellect in one of the leading politicians of the country, Lord Metroland, results only in such "hand-to-mouth thinking" as this? He has been told at a party that the mad antics of the younger generation result from a "radical instability" in the country. Somewhat puzzled and concerned, he returns to his mansion to find his drunken stepson, Peter Pastmaster, fumbling with the lock. To his greeting Peter's only answer, repeated several times, is "Oh, go to hell." Seeing a tall hat on the table by the door, Metroland concludes that it belongs to his wife's lover, Alastair Digby-Vaine-Trumpington, and goes into the study because "it would be awkward if he met young Trumpington on the stairs." Once in his study he surveys the familiar details: the businesslike arrangement of the furniture, the solid green safe with the brass handle, and the rows of comforting books which promise knowledge and security: *Who's Who,* the *Encyclopedia Britannica, Debrett, The Dictionary of National Biography*. These reassure him greatly, and when he hears Trumpington leaving he says to himself, "radical instability indeed," and goes upstairs to his beautiful aristocratic wife, whose wealth comes from the operation of a chain of South American brothels.

Such vacuity—and Metroland is a *thinker* compared to most of Waugh's characters—justifies Waugh's unstated but insistent argument that a meaningful society can only be one which follows and defends strenuously some

8

traditional pattern of belief and value. If people cannot reason clearly or feel deeply—and there is no indication in Waugh's novel that the majority of them ever could— then their only hope of a full and valuable life is to follow the traditions evolved during the long course of trial and error which is human history. Leave man, individual man, to decide on his own values, throw him into a relativistic world in which nothing is certain, corrupt the traditional institutions and ways of doing things so that no honest man can believe in them, and the result will be, as Waugh regularly shows, confusion, self-defeat, the grotesque distortion of human nature, and frantic but meaningless activity.

It is the arrangement of incidents and the overall pattern of events—plot—which ultimately establish the "meaning" in Waugh's novels. Like most satires, they lack a conventional story, intricately contrived and carefully followed. The sporadic attempts of two young people to get married, a picaresque ramble through English society, occasional references to the decay of a marriage, these and other such devices loosely bind the incidents together. But the books are not constructed around these plot lines, for what in more conventionally constructed novels would be the main story appears only now and then. When it does the situation will often have changed considerably since its last appearance, but no explanation is offered of how these changes came about. The effect is of something "just happening," of a discontinuity through which some unknown and unidentifiable power is working to force matters to a disastrous conclusion.

The major portion of the satires is composed of a series of brief and apparently unrelated episodes which flash on the pages in the manner of scenes from a newsreel. A scene in a fashionable London restaurant will be followed by a meal in the African or Brazilian jungles; a business journey will be interrupted by a long, carefully reported conversation between two women—neither of whom we have ever seen before or see again—about a recent scandal at Ten Downing Street. Events at a boys' school will give way to a discussion of modern architecture by a Professor Otto Silenus. Even when Waugh follows for a considerable length of time the adventures of the same characters, they will move at random from watching a movie being made, to a party, to an automobile race, stopping along the way to have a number of drinks, look for a hotel room, drive through a slum in the industrial Midlands. Then the scene flickers to another setting and we are watching the ridiculous pretensions of a sister in a fashionable nursing home, listening to a gossip columnist telephone his editor, and hearing about a young boy who fell out of an airplane.

By some standards Waugh would appear to have put his novels together very badly, but he is, of course, reproducing in his arrangement of scenes and his handling of time the chaotic, frenetic, disconnected movements of modern life. Only a true culture, not a disintegrating one, can have an Aristotelian plot in which one event follows inevitably from another and the whole is composed of a beginning, a middle, and an end. But randomness and disorganization are only surface effects. Each of the episodes is thematically related to the others with which it is in sequence. All show in different terms the assault of appetite and stupidity, the ravening tiger and the ponderous elephant, on the old beliefs and ways of life, and the consequent meaninglessness. The scenes are carefully arranged so that one scene defines its neighbors: an episode of polite savagery in London is juxtaposed to a scene of overt savagery in the jungle, or a description of an ultra-modern house built for machines rather than men borders on a party scene in which fashionable men and women move in a pattern of conditioned responses and respond to every new situation with the predictability of a machine.

Satire regularly offers not a still, quiet world but a busy, bustling one in which crowds of men race furiously about pursuing some *ignis fatuus*. In Waugh's satires railway lines are thrown across primitive wastes, huge business empires are in ceaseless movement creating new products and searching for new markets, busy factories cover the landscape, and cars race madly about the roads. Solemn, serious politicians, educators, clergymen, financiers, and men of affairs move confidently forward on the path of change, progress, and enlightened self-interest. The disillusioned younger generation rushes restlessly about in search of pleasure and something new in life. Amiable rogues endlessly move on looking for new amusements and more profitable deals. This is, on the surface, the humming, vigorous world of the twentieth century, the era of ceaseless change and inevitable progress. But all this movement is illusory, for in Waugh's world, as in Carroll's Wonderland, "it takes all the running you can do to keep in the same place."

What in fact happens in Waugh's novels is that all the running produces only circular movement—the second of the patterns Swift shows to result from self-delusive flights, overreaching fancy, which go "like one who travels the East into West; or like a strait line drawn by its own length into a Circle." The circle has been in the past a figure of perfection, but it has also been, as it is in Dante's *Inferno,* the figure of empty, meaningless movement, of eternal hunger which never finds satisfaction or rest. It is in this "infernal" sense that circularity appears in Waugh. It is the pattern of aimless, self-defeating life, the natural movement of the jungle and the savage:

Dancing was resumed, faster this time and more clearly oblivious of fatigue. In emulation of the witch doctors the tribesmen began slashing themselves on chest and arms with their hunting knives; blood and sweat mingled in shining rivulets over their dark skins. Now and then one of them would pitch forward on to his face and lie panting or roll stiff in a nervous seizure. Women joined in the dance, making another chain, circling in the reverse way to the men. They were dazed with drink, stamping themselves into ecstasy. The two chains jostled and combined. They shuffled together interlocked.

The English spectator at this dance draws back dazed from the heat of the fire, the monotonous sound of the drums, and the mind-obliterating circular movement of the dance; but the man of the future, the hypercivilized Professor Otto Silenus, who looks forward to the day when men will be as functional as machines and houses as simple in design as factories, finds the circle the only true image of life:

It's like the big wheel at Luna Park. . . . You pay five francs and go into a room with tiers of seats all around, and in the centre the floor is made of polished wood that revolves quickly. At first you sit down and watch the others. They are all trying to sit in the wheel, and they keep getting flung off, and that makes them laugh, and you laugh too. . . . the nearer you can get to the hub of the wheel the slower it is moving and the easier it is to stay on. There's generally someone in the centre who stands up and sometimes does a sort of dance. Often he's paid by the management though. . . . Of course at the very centre there's a point completely at rest, if one could only find it. . . . Lots of people just enjoy scrambling on and being whisked off and scrambling on again. . . . Then there are others . . . who sit as far out as they can and hold on for dear life. . . . the scrambling and excitement and bumps and the effort to get to the middle, and when we do get to the middle, it's just as if we never started. It's so odd.

The jungle dance and the wheel at Luna Park are the two extremes which meet, primitive past and primitive future, the blood-crazed circling of the stone-age savage and the mechanical construction of a technologically advanced civilization without humane direction. These are the two great images of the hopeless circle in which existence moves in Waugh's world, but the circular pattern appears everywhere. Politics is a circular game. The Right Honourable Walter Outrage M.P. is in one week as Prime Minister and out the next, and it is an attentive man who can tell at any given moment whether Outrage is in or out. The bright young things in search of amusement go to an endless series of parties, parties in hospitals, parties in hotels, masked parties, savage parties, parties in stately old houses, parties in bed, but all parties turn out to be the same party where one hears the same talk and sees the same faces. Waugh's trick, deriving from Thackeray, of having the same people with the same ridiculous names pop up again and again in the most unlikely places makes it appear that it is impossible to break out of this circle of familiars. And when these people do pop up they are always doing the same old things. Lady Metralond is always suggesting to attractive young girls that if they are dissatisfied with their present situation a position can be found for them as entertainers in Buenos Aires. Lord Monomark is still surrounded by several perfect beauties and several sycophants listening to him talk about his latest fad diet. Peter Pastmaster is still drunk, Alastair Digby-Vaine-Trumpington is still drinking, and the mysterious Toby Crutwell—sometime cat burglar, war hero, and M.P.—has still left the party just before we arrived. *The Daily Excess* and *The Daily Beast* are still getting the news wrong, the older generation is still worried about the younger, Parsnip and Pimpernell are still writing left-wing poetry and issuing manifestoes, and Basil Seal is still managing to get money out of someone.

Each novel describes a circular movement. *Decline and Fall* follows the adventures of that young innocent, Paul Pennyfeather, sent down from Scone College for running pantless across the quadrangle after being debagged by the Bollinger Club. In his search for a living he first takes a position as a master in a boys' school, Llanabba Castle, run as a private venture by Augustus Fagan, Ph.D. Falling in love with Margot Beste-Chetwynde, the mother of one of his students, he follows her into the fashionable world of London society. Just before they are to be married, she sends him on a business trip to Marseilles to clear up some difficulties about the transportation of several girls to her South American enterprises. Paul, completely unaware of the nature of this business, is shadowed by a League of Nations representative—an old college chum named Potts—and later arrested. Sentenced to a long term

13

in jail, he is later rescued by Margot who buys him out by agreeing to marry Metroland, the Home Secretary. A bogus death is arranged at a nursing home run by Dr. Fagan, and later Paul returns to Scone to resume his "education." He uses the same name, explaining that he is the cousin of the deceased Pennyfeather, and grows a moustache. As the book ends Paul has just returned from listening to a paper on the Polish plebiscites, the subject of the paper he had listened to on the fateful evening when he was caught by the Boller. Outside there is "a confused roaring and breaking of glass." The Bollinger Club is again holding its annual meeting.

What starts as a linear progress, a picaresque journey, through the various levels of English society gradually takes the shape of a great circle, the wheel in Luna Park described by Professor Silenus. Men and women scramble frantically over its surface, dancing, cavorting, grimly seeking the center, or just spinning dizzily for the ride. But they get nowhere. As the wheel turns we see different aspects of English society, but as each new scene turns into view it becomes but another version of what we have already found elsewhere. These recurring forms of dullness have sometimes different, sometimes the same names. Augustus Fagan, Ph.D., first appears running a pretentious school to make money, and he ends running a shabby nursing home and arranging false death certificates to make money. Prendergast is first the minister who, while sitting one day in his pleasant house with the chintz curtains put up by his mother, is suddenly unable to understand "why God made the world at all." He is next a master at a school where he is unable to discipline the boys and cannot teach them anything because he has nothing to teach. Then he crops up as a Modern Churchman—"who draws the full salary of a beneficed clergyman and need not commit himself to any religious belief"—and the Chaplain of the prison to which Paul is sent. Here he has the same trouble with the prisoners that he had with the boys and ends, appropriately enough, as the victim of the mad carpenter. His fate serves also to demonstrate the disordering effects in church, school, and prison of the loss of belief in a more general sense. In every place this and similar disordering powers—savagery, greed, pomposity, ignorance, and idealism so simple-minded as to be criminal—crop up in character after character, and their recurrence turns every scene into the same scene. College, school, prison, the Ritz are all the same places, governed by the same people, for the same purposes. Perhaps the only change in the novel occurs in Paul who, having died and been reborn, has lost his simple-minded beliefs about the natural goodness of human nature and the perfectibility of man and come to share Waugh's view of the necessity of a rigidly enforced social order. Upon returning to Scone and hearing in a lecture of a heretical second-century bishop who "denied the divinity of Christ, the immortality of the soul, the existence of good, the legality of marriage, and the validity of the Sacrament of Extreme Unction"—all the values denied in the giddy world through which he has passed—Paul can only reflect with satisfaction, "How right they had been to condemn him!"

Vile Bodies is a panorama of the life of the "bright young people" of the late '20's and their disapproving elders. The scenes of the novel are gathered loosely around the engagement of Adam Fenwick-Symes and Nina Blount, which is now on, now off, now on, as Adam seeks, finds, and then loses the money which would enable them to marry. Giddy as they are, their marriage still represents the search for a traditional way of life which in many ways all the younger people of the book restlessly seek—and desperately need. But you need money to marry, and so money comes to represent the support offered both by society to those who seek entrance to it and by the older generation to those who will share and perpetuate their values. Adam first tries to earn the necessary money, the emblematic support, by writing his autobiography, but officious, ignorant customs officials destroy his manuscript as pornography. Adam turns then for money to the business world and is forced to sign a "very simple" contract with the publishers Rampole and Benfleet: "No royalty on the first two thousand, then a royalty of two and a half per cent., rising to five per cent. on the tenth thousand. We retain serial, cinema, dramatic, American, Colonial, and translation rights, of course. And, of course, an option on your next twelve books on the same terms. It's a very straightforward arrangement really. Doesn't leave room for any of the disputes which embitter the relations of author and publisher." Just as the empty, adulterous marriages of the older generation offer no moral support for Adam's and Nina's marriage, so there is no financial support forthcoming from their families. Adam travels down to see Colonel Blount, Nina's father and the master of Doubting Hall—usually pronounced Doubting 'All by the natives—a half-witted but cunning old eccentric who spends all his time sleeping and eating. Lately Colonel Blount has found a passion for the "silver screen" and in hopes of getting a big part he has financed a fantastic horse-opera version of the life of John Wesley which has been filmed at his house. When Adam asks him for money the old man responds cheerfully with a check for a thousand pounds, signed "Charlie Chaplin."

His identity destroyed with his autobiography, his hope of making a living by writing turned to economic slavery, and all possibility of support from the older generation and traditional social arrangements obliterated, Adam and Nina can only trust themselves to Fortune and her turning wheel. They begin a joyless little affair, and Fortune then arrives in the person of a drunk major to whom Adam entrusts a thousand pounds he has just won in an idiotic bet. The money is to be placed on a horse named Indian Runner. The horse wins, but for the remainder of the book Adam and the drunk Major chase one another around trying to collect or give away 35,000 pounds, though it is never quite certain whether the Major really has the money or whether he has simply bilked Adam. Each time the fortune seems within Adam's grasp the marriage to

Nina is on, each time he loses sight of the Major it is off. No Juliet—Waugh's characters are always rather deficient in love—Nina finally marries a wealthy young boor named Ginger Littlejohn but immediately recommences the affair with Adam, even passing him off as her husband on a Christmas visit to Doubting 'All. When Adam and the Major finally do complete their tranaction it is on the enormous wasteland of the greatest battlefield in history where the book ends; but the 35,000 devalued pounds are only worth a couple of drinks and a newspaper. Nina is still married to Ginger, but about to bear Adam's child, and all the other nincompoops of the book are carrying on in their usual way.

Most of the scenes in *Vile Bodies* deal with the varied activities of the other "bright young people," Miles Malpractice, Agatha Runcible, Archie Schwert, and Mary Mouse. They have, like Adam and Nina, committed themselves to Fortune because everything in their world is, in their language, "too, too bogus." They reel from party to party, body to body, and binge to binge, racing faster and faster after an elusive something which always escapes them. And because they have lost their bearings they travel in endless circles. The dizzying circularity of their movements is objectified in the motor races, the great scene of the book. These dirt-track races are held in the Midlands near a grimy industrial city, where a vast crowd, fascinated with speed and hoping for bloodshed, gathers to watch the "Speed Kings" go round and round. But the real Speed Kings are the bright young people whose mad races are reported daily to the sensation-hungry readers of the press, and it is inevitable that one of them will find her way into the race. Dead drunk and mistakenly wearing a spare driver's brassard, Agatha Runcible ends up behind the wheel of the English entry, a Plunkett-Bowse. After a few magnificent whirls around the course she speeds off into the countryside until losing control of the car she runs head on into a market cross. She later dies in a delirium still shouting, "Faster, faster."

Black Mischief is essentially the story of the arch-rogue Basil Seal and of Seth, "Emperor of Azania, Chief of Chiefs of the Sakuyu, Lord of the Wanda and Tyrant of the Seas, Bachelor of the Arts of Oxford University." Azania is a thinly disguised version of Abyssinia, which Waugh visited as a reporter twice during the 1930's. The book turns on Seth's random attempts to make of Azania a model state and to impose on his savage people those modern ways of thought, institutions, and hard goods which romantic liberals once believed would bring about the reform of society and the perfection of man: paper money, birth control, boots for the Imperial Guard, woman suffrage, architecture, and Esperanto. The local population offers considerable resistance to such innovations —the guardsmen eat the boots—and when they do accept the new ideas they somehow get them all wrong. They think, for example, that birth control and its apparatus— which is known as "The Emperor's juju"—will provide them with immense numbers of children, and so they march proudly in the *Place Marie Stopes* under the brave banner, "Through Sterility to Culture." Most readers have considered, wrongly, that *Black Mischief* is a brutal and unjustified satire on the stupidity of the black races and their comical mangling of Western ideas and institutions. Some elements of racial chauvinism are unavoidably here, but the main thrust of the satire is against Western liberals who believe that life can be utterly reformed, anywhere, by increased control over nature and the change of social institutions. Waugh makes this point very cleverly, and very consistently, by such means as juxtaposing similar scenes in Africa and England, by showing the same forces at work in both places.

Black Mischief is not primarily a caricature of a savage and ludicrous African kingdom but a grotesque image of Western civilization in the twentieth century. Where in his earlier books Waugh sends his characters into only figurative jungles of English society, he now sends Seth and Basil Seal into an actual jungle where cannibalism becomes a reality and the barbarians really do file their teeth, not just their tongues and wits. The apostles of jungle progress, the crude profiteers, the ludicrous aristocracy, and the cannibals of Azania are but extensions of attitudes and people who appear in more normal clothes and speak in more familiar accents in the novels set in England.

Here as in England life runs in great meaningless circles. At the center deep in the Azanian jungle Basil Seal buries the murdered Emperor and Bachelor of the Arts of Oxford University who has thought to abolish savagery and darkness by fiat, technology, education, and Swedish exercises. The drums throb in the funeral ceremony, round and round goes the maddened dance until even that shape cannot hold and the dance disintegrates into grunting couples on the ground in the darkness. Out of the stew-pot and into Basil's stomach comes the unrecognised flesh of Prudence Courteney, his mistress and the silly daughter of the even sillier English envoy to Azania, who because he believed that all the threats of trouble would "no doubt blow over," literally tended to his knitting, and never concerned himself with politics or his official duties. Out beyond these circles there are others which look less barbaric only because they are more familiar. *Black Mischief* begins with a description of the Portuguese attempts to colonize Azania in the fifteenth century, describes the later invasion of the Arabs, and then in succession the rise to power of a Wanda chief, Seth's progressive administration, and the establishment of a protectorate by the French and English. This looks like what is called progress: paved roads, neat administrative bungalows, clean water supply, lighted and policed streets. But it is in fact only another form of the old power game, and back in the jungle the drums still beat and the tribesmen still tear up the railroad irons for spear heads and rip down telegraph lines to make copper bracelets for their women. In the middle of the main thoroughfare of town a family, which no government has been able to move, still squats in a wrecked car, and in the markets the age-old racket of selling junk to the government goes on. *Plus ça change, plus c'est la même chose.* After his cannibal feast Basil Seal returns to the savages of London and finds them still doing the same things they were doing when he left. Azania fades from sight with the comforting music of Gilbert and Sullivan floating out over the waters which lap continuously at the seawall.

"Is it weakness of intellect, birdie," I cried,
"Or a rather tough worm in your little inside?"

a question to which Waugh's satires give the most un-Victorian answer, "Both."

A Handful of Dust also gives the illusion of a developing plot. It begins with another of Waugh's havens of innocence: Hetton, a huge Victorian Gothic house which is the family home of the Lasts. Tony Last, the present owner, is an English gentleman raised in the humane tradition. He is deeply attached to his home, cares for the tenantry long after it has ceased to be economical to do so, is seriously concerned with new farming methods and improving the land, loves his wife and only son, has charming manners, and goes to church every week, though he has no religious beliefs. Tony Last is, as Waugh once pointed out, a "humanist," and his old-fashioned, nineteenth-century dream of a "City of Man" held together by good sense and warm hearts finds its architectural expression in the grotesquely attractive Victorian Gothic Hetton, which is, significantly, a reconstruction of an older, more beautiful Hetton Abbey. The present Hetton's heavy battlements, clock tower, armorial stained glass, huge brass and wrought-iron gasolier, and pitch-pine mistrels' gallery, whatever their peculiar historical interest, were no more than a dream of chivalry and ancient values when the building was constructed in the 1860's with money earned from the cotton mills, collieries, and furnaces of Coketown. The simple, economic impracticality of Hetton in the twentieth century is apparent in the impossibility of keeping it in repair, staffing it, or heating it after paying death duties and estate taxes. The naïveté of the social and moral values it expresses in glazed brick and encaustic tile is apparent in the names given its bedrooms—Yseult, Elaine, Modred, Gawain, Lancelot, and Guinevere — by men who read Tennyson rather than Malory. Year after year as the dream becomes smaller and smaller, room after room is closed off.

In Waugh's world such a dream, no matter how attractive it may appear, is doomed, for its romantic failure to face reality squarely provides no walls against the inevitable attacks of savagery and ignorance. Tony Last's amusing and beautiful wife, Brenda, bored with life at Hetton, conceives an inexplicable and uncontrolled passion for a bloodless, self-centered young man, John Beaver, and leaves Hetton to plunge into the polite cruelty of London social life. Each weekend she returns and looses a new group of modern savages on Hetton, interior decorators, spiritualists, international fancy women, young gigolos, and fashionable sponges. Each week she drains more money from Hetton to support her young man and pay for her pleasures. There is no planned malice in this, only a kind of mindless cruelty, which is matched in nature by a highly-bred and poorly trained horse who kicks Tony's only child, John Andrew, to death at a hunt.

This brings the marriage to an end, and Brenda demands a divorce and all the money Tony needs to run Hetton. He refuses and is subjected to a series of unbelievable indignities. But even after all this he cannot give up his dream of The City: "the Shining, the Many Watered, the Bright Feathered, the Aromatic Jam. He had a clear picture of it in his mind. It was Gothic in character, all vanes and pinnacles, gargoyles, battlements, groining and tracery, pavilions and terraces, a transfigured Hetton, pennons and banners floating on the sweet breeze, everything luminous and translucent; a coral citadel crowning a green hilltop with daisies, among groves and streams; a tapestry landscape filled with heraldic and fabulous animals and symmetrical, disproportionate blossoms." Led on by tales of a lost city, Tony plunges into the Brazilian jungle still in search of his dream. But the fabled city turns out also to be an illusion, and with his guide dead Tony wanders feverishly through the jungle to fall at last into the hands of an unquestionable madman, the illiterate half-caste Todd, who lives in isolation in a clearing in the jungle. Todd's father, a missionary from Barbados turned gold prospector, left him a complete set of Dickens which he loves to have read to him, and he holds Tony prisoner forcing him to read again and again those sentimental stories—which, like Hetton, express the Victorian, humane vision of life—in which villains always die and intelligent little boys and pure young women after periods of trial and suffering win through at last to peace, prosperity, and the discovery of their rightful names and heritages.

The wheel has come full circle once again, with the difference that Tony is now condemned to live his life out reading over and over his dream of life in a setting which makes clear that it is nothing but a dream. At the opening of *A Handful of Dust* the fiction embodied in the architecture of Hetton, Brenda's familiar face and kind voice, and the peaceful round of daily life concealed from Tony the fact that he lived not among the "happy circle of loved faces," but under "the harsh glare of an alien sun" among the "ravening tiger and the exotic camel, the furtive jackal and the ponderous elephant." At the end he can stare into the mad eyes of Mr. Todd and look at the tangled jungle and empty waste around him and see the truth. But on and on he must go, reading again and again of how all turns out well because the human heart is good and kind.

In Waugh's first novel, *Decline and Fall,* there is a remarkably fine comic description of the Annual School Sports at Llanabba Castle. The stated purpose of the meet is, of course, to encourage and test the endurance, courage, and physical skills of the young gentlemen being educated at Llanabba. The actual purpose is to impress and gratify, by allowing their sons to win, several important visiting parents. Since the parsimonious daughter of the headmaster has burned the high and low hurdles for firewood during the winter—and the spiked railings provided as substitutes are at length declared unsuitable—the major events of the meet are the foot races. Dr. Fagan, the headmaster, has stated firmly that he is not interested in the details of the races but in "style," and very stylish the fete is, with champagne cup, masses of flowers, a pavillion, elaborately printed programs, and the Llandudno Silver Band ceaselessly playing "Men of Harlech." But there is no track, no distance markers are set out, and no decision has been made about the distance of the races. The boys chosen to race for the delight of their parents are simply lined up and told to run to a clump of trees and back again. They are going to go on racing "until it is time for tea." Mr. Prendergast, the master serving as starter, is dead drunk and fires his first shot into one of the boys, little Lord Tangent. Tangent is carried off, and around and around go the boys to the encouraging shouts of "Well run, Percy!" and "Jolly good race," and the unceasing noise of the Llandudno Silver Band. One boy, young Clutterbuck, the son of the local brewer, simply omits a lap by hiding behind the trees, and when at last the race is brought to a conclusion by the arrival of the most important guests and the beginning of tea, he "breasts the tape" well ahead of the others. When the win is disputed, Dr. Fagan easily settles the matter by declaring Clutterbuck the winner of the five furlongs race, "a very exacting length," while the other boys are called the winner and runners-up in the three miles, another "exacting length." The prizes for the winners in these remarkable games are, fittingly enough, awarded by Lady Circumference.

In his description of the revolutionary government of Mexico in the 1930's, *Robbery Under Law,* Waugh remarks that he does not believe that there is any one God-given form of government, but that a government consistent in its principles and dedicated to keeping order is necessary because "given propitious circumstances, men and women who seem quite orderly, will commit every conceivable atrocity. The danger does not come merely from habitual hooligans; we are all potential recruits for anarchy. Unremitting effort is needed to keep men living together at peace; there is only a margin left over for experiment however beneficent." Lacking *consistent* principles and failing to keep the peace results in those meaningless, endless circles around which his characters run in his novels. Once the boundaries, the rules, and the markers are destroyed, as they are at the Llanabba races, then the rational judgment no longer has a framework within which to locate and identify things, and the purpose of human effort is lost. Cupidity, pride, stupidity, and cunning are loosed to complete the wreckage of order and obliterate the meaning of any dimly remembered purpose. However, running round and round until tea time and the arrival of the most important guest was no doubt the best possible training for boys about to enter the giddy whirl of Waugh's world where all rules are off, all the markers gone, all races shams because there is no longer any sense of being a "creature with a defined purpose."

Charles E. Linck, Jr.

THE PUBLIC VIEW OF WAUGH'S CONVERSION

Death prevented Evelyn Waugh from continuing his auto-biography to the point of his reception into the Roman Catholic Church on September 29, 1930, but judging from his reticence about his subject's spiritual life in the Knox biography, he would probably have left us little the wiser about his own inner life. In his best-known statement about his conversion, [1] he stressed the historical and logical arguments that led him to Rome and took some pains to refute notions that he might have been influenced by emotion or by social or aesthetic considerations. There is no reason to doubt his sincerity or his accuracy, but these and other later accounts give little sense of the complexity of his motives or the interest that his conversion aroused. For his contemporaries, it was a newsworthy event, primarily social rather than religious in its implications. Waugh's response to this attention showed that he was far from being a Mayfair butterfly and revealed something about the importance of religion in his view of society and of history.

Sometime after his divorce, Waugh began taking instructions from Father Martin D'Arcy, S.J., one of the more eminent Farm Street Jesuits, to whom he had been referred by his friends the Plunkett-Greenes. [2] His conversion was foreshadowed by an "Author's Note" in *Labels* to the effect that his views on Catholicism had "developed and changed in many ways" since he had writ-

From "The Development of Evelyn Waugh's Career: 1903-1939," unpublished dissertation, University of Kansas, 1962. Reprinted by permission of the author.

ten the book. *Labels* appeared on September 25; five days later, Lord Beaverbrook's *Daily Express*—which was to be a kind of journalistic sponsor at Waugh's conversion —carried the headline, "Another Author Turns to Rome, Mr. Evelyn Waugh Leaves Church of England, Young Satirist of Mayfair." [3] The article beneath put him in distinguished company:

His action provides yet another instance of a remarkable tendency among British authors in recent years.

It is rather less than a year since Miss Sheila Kaye-Smith and her husband entered the Church of Rome.

Mr. Compton MacKenzie entered during the war, and Mr. Alfred Noyes, the poet, in 1927. The Hon. Evan Morgan, heir to a peerage and a wealthy amateur of letters, was received in 1919.

The Hon. Maurice Baring, Father Ronald Knox, and Mr. G. K. Chesterton are other distinguished literary Roman Catholics. [4]

The story was supplemented by an editorial, "A Roman Catholic Convert," for *The Daily Express* wanted to proselytize as well as inform:

Another British author has been received into the Roman Catholic Church. In this case the author is hardly more than a boy, and his writing suggests an almost passionate adherence to the ultra-modern. Yet he turns, as so many novelists have done since the war, to the Church that does not alter with the years.

Is it that the post-war novelists seek refuge from their own writings, that deal so exclusively with their queer little cocktail world? Or is it that the swiftly changing conditions of today create a universal longing for permanency, for a Church that refuses to do honour to compromise? Whatever the answer, these are questions worthy of consideration by every priest who wears God's uniform. [5]

The *Express* appeared to associate, in a sympathetic manner, this "trend" with its exasperated fear of the loss of Empire, and other signs of degeneration. The Beaverbrook *Evening Standard* was much sterner in its more conservative gossip column, "The Londoner's Diary," and offered another explanation:

Mr. Evelyn Waugh has been received into the Roman Church by Father D'Arcy. This announcement will not come as a surprise to his admirers. . . . Mr. Waugh will now join that cohort of Roman satirists which has gone over to the Roman Church. There is no reason why the summer lightning of his fantasy should in any way be dimmed.

Perhaps his conversion may even prevent Mr. Waugh from taking too seriously his own disillusions. Somewhere round the corner of his brilliance has lurked the grim figure of calvinism. This figure may now be exorcised. [6]

Less solemn gossip writers also recorded the event. "Dragoman" gave a sketch of Waugh the social satirist looking down on a cafe crowd in Coventry Street:

Here . . . were Lady Ravendale, lately back from Russia, but wearing an exquisitely capitalist evening dress; and Miss Tallulah Bankhead, who was with the Hon. David Herbert; and the Marquis de Casa Maury; and, watching critically from the balcony, Mr. Evelyn Waugh, who had earlier in the evening been received into the Roman Catholic Church. [7]

One letter from a reader was published; it praised the Beaverbrook press for its "freedom and liberty" in displaying such news and offered a condemnation of the "unchanging Church." [8] In a society magazine there was a photograph by J. Maycock of Waugh with a ragged "crew-cut," a tie and collar awry, a pout on the mouth; its caption lumped all the literary converts together. [9] An item such as this may have made readers think there had been a landslide of conversions; there was not.

The Daily Express was not finished with the matter. After Waugh had left for Abyssinia, it featured in a large first page announcement: "My conversion to Rome, by Evelyn Waugh, the young novelist, A Striking Article, See Page 10 Today." Covering two-thirds of the editorial page, Waugh's article was prominently headlined: " 'Converted to Rome, Why it Happened to me,' by Evelyn Waugh, whose novels have brought him fame at 26." [10] An editor's note expressed the opinion that it was "a well-thought-out article" which "explains why he took the momentous step."

Waugh began with the statement that "three popular errors reappear with depressing regularity in any discussion about a convert to the Roman Catholic Church." These errors were "the Jesuits have got hold of him," "he is captivated by the Ritual," and "he wants to have his mind made up for him." He denied that these "errors" applied in his instance, and explained or qualified the charges to fit his conversion; it was a revealing article. The Jesuits were not a "spiritual press-gang," the Church of England had actual advantage in church buildings and English prose, and the "Roman system can and does form a basis for the most vigorous intellectual and artistic activity." If the Roman Church was recruiting many "who are not notably gullible, dull-witted, or eccentric," he had an explanation:

It seems to me that in the present phase of European history, the essential issue is no longer between Catholicism, on one side, and Protestantism, on the other, but between Christianity and Chaos.

Waugh's explanation was elaborated in the manner that Hilaire Belloc and T. S. Eliot had used before; but Waugh's statement about Western civilization's "loss of Faith" was readably direct:

Today we can see it on all sides as the active negation of all that Western culture has stood for. *Civilization*—and by this I do not mean talking cinemas and tinned food, nor even surgery and hygienic houses, but the whole moral and artistic organization of Europe—has not in itself the power of survival. It came into being through Christianity, and without it has no significance or power to command allegiance.

The loss of faith in Christianity and the consequent lack of confidence in moral and social standards have become embodied in the ideal of a materialistic, mechanized state, already existent in Russia and rapidly spreading south and west.

28

The Prayer Book controversy, the recent Lambeth Conference, and the newspaper articles of Dean Inge [11] and other Modern Churchmen had apparently played a part:

In the Anglican Church today matters of supreme importance in faith and morals are still discussed indecisively, while the holders of high office are able to make public assertions which do violence to the deepest feelings of many of their people. [12]

The latter statement shows that his attention to the problem was not caused altogether by recent personal disturbances. Then, too, his travels earlier in the Mediterranean had helped to change his convictions:

No one visiting a Roman Catholic country can fail to be struck by the fact that the people do use their churches. It is not a matter of going to a service on Sunday; all classes at all hours of the day can be seen dropping in on their way to and from their work. . . . You never see in Roman Catholics going to Mass, as one sees on the faces of many people going to Chapel, that look of being rather better than their neighbors.

The Protestant attitude seems to be, 'I am good; therefore I go to Church,' while the Catholic's is, 'I am far from being good; therefore I go to Church.'

Aside from the last part of his article, which provoked sharp response from letter writers, this was a standard statement without being in any way insincere; Waugh wrote what others had written at greater length. Overall, the article seems to bear out Father D'Arcy's repeated statements that Waugh had long been searching into the problem of religion (though oftentimes his publicized acts might have seemed to belie this) and that he demanded the most rigorous intellectual presentation of the defenses for the Roman Church's possession of the truth. [13]

Perhaps it would be useful to attempt a distinction about the quality of that intellectual rigor. On his trip to the Mediterranean in 1928 he had rejected several Eastern cultures on aesthetic grounds; on Crete aesthetic rejection was mingled with moral disgust. His enthusiasm in *Labels* for the great unfinished Catholic Church that Gaudi had begun in Barcelona as well as his subdued but evident change of temper about Roman churches during several other stops in Spain make *Labels* and the trip itself the significant prelude to his conversion. Aesthetic emotion entered in. Other facts that point to something more modified than a *logical* conviction are that the Plunkett-Greenes were sympathetically related to the Roman Catholic "Modernist" Baron von Hugel; that Maud Plunkett-Greene's *Mount Zion* (1929) [14] which Waugh referred to as an influence, though providing a few topical contrasts between the Church of England and the Roman Catholic Church, is essentially a religious-emotion charged manual for contemplative thought; that Father D'Arcy was then engaged with writing his *Nature of Belief* (issued September, 1931) which synthesized the "Modernist" notions of conversion by "inner light" with intellectual-rational conviction and was therefore a powerful apologist for conversion in which aesthetic sense vied with reason on equal terms. Father D'Arcy's *Nature of Belief,* for instance, convinced Evelyn Underhill in her *Spectator* review that it was dangerous to read his book at all:

In a final chapter . . . Father D'Arcy passes from the levels of belief endorsed by reason, to the supernatural certitudes of faith. Here, as he acknowledges, he seems to take a "flying leap". . . . Those who make this jump under Father D'Arcy's guidance, will hardly feel surprised that it brings them to earth well within the frontiers of the Vatican State. [15]

It is difficult, therefore, to understand the "firm intellectual conviction but . . . little emotion" with which Waugh was converted. [16] There seems, on the contrary, to have been sufficient cause for an emotional — part of which was an aesthetically emotional—impulse toward the "unchanging Church." Further, it has been remarked that Waugh knew he was being practical: "After he had been converted to Rome, he told me that its attitude to divorce would keep him from the folly of marrying again." [17] His unhappiness about his marriage was a palpable basic cause, [18] no matter how calm his explanation in *The Daily Express*. Therefore, it is possible to conjecture that Waugh's movement toward Catholicism was not entirely free from emotional and aesthetic impulses although these were overshadowed and to a considerable degree supplanted by intellectual and historical grounds for belief.

NOTES

1 "Come Inside," *The Road to Damascus,* ed. John O'Brien (New York: Image Books, Doubleday & Co., Inc., 1955,) pp. 6-7.

2 Unpublished letter of M. C. D'Arcy, S.J., to Charles Linck, August 22, 1961.

3 *Daily Express,* September 30, 1930, p. 1.

4 *Ibid.*

5 *Ibid.,* p. 8.

6 "Evelyn Waugh," *Evening Standard,* September 30, 1930, p. 6.

7 *Daily Express,* October 1, 1930, p. 15.

8 *Daily Express,* October 4, 1930, p. 8.

9 *Bystander,* October 8, 1930, p. 101.

10 *Daily Express,* October 20, 1930, pp. 1, 10.

11 For example "Amazing Marriage Suggestions by Dean Inge, Plea for 'Limited Contracts,' Wedded—But Not For Life, No Church Blessing, Unions 'that the State Should Recognize,'" *Daily Express,* September 11, 1930, p. 1 [an article about Inge's *Christian Ethics and Modern Problems*]. Dean Inge's weekly column in *The Evening Standard* was controversial in 1930.

12 *Daily Express,* October 20, 1930, p. 10.

13 Unpublished letters of M. C. D'Arcy, S.J., to Charles Linck, June 20, 1960, and August 22, 1961. Of interest is the following: "In the gay company of Oxford, Mayfair, Paris and the South of France, he led a life of intense personal piety and was converted to Roman Catholicism in 1930." (Editorial Note to "Fan-Fare," *Life,* XX [April 8, 1946], 53.)

14 Maud Plunkett-Greene, a sister of Elizabeth Ponsonby's mother and mother to David, Richard, and Olivia, whom

Evelyn knew well, was received into the Roman Church in 1926 (*Catholic Who's Who and Year Book*. London: Burns, Oates and Washbourne, 1931). She dedicated her book to "My Daughter Olivia," whom Evelyn had liked very much indeed.

15 September 12, 1931, p. 391.

16 "Come Inside."

17 Unpublished letter of Terence Greenidge to Charles Linck, October 25, 1961.

18 See Alex Waugh, *My Brother Evelyn and Other Portraits* (New York: Farrar, Straus, & Giroux, Inc., 1967), pp. 191-197.

Patricia Corr

EVELYN WAUGH: SANITY AND CATHOLICISM

Much of the early criticism of Mr. Waugh's novels tended
to concentrate on particular and often superficial aspects
of his writing. He was justly lauded as a brilliant satirist,
the laureate of the Gay Twenties, and condemned as a
cruel joker or a snob whose myopic view of Society was
confined to the Mayfair set known as the Bright Young
People. Recent criticism is more perceptive. 'The Mask
of the social satirist in Mr. Waugh,' writes Mr. F. J. Stopp
in his definitive work *Evelyn Waugh. Portrait of an Artist,*
'only partially conceals the features of the moralist.' I pro-
pose in this article to unmask the reveller, to investigate
the serious undertones thinly disguised in Mr. Waugh's
novels. Mr. Waugh is both a sound moralist and an ob-
servant humorist and it is his humour which makes pal-
atable the unpleasant medicines he prescribes for his
readers.

The world depicted in the novels is one of seemingly
irreparable futility. It is a sham world of hypocrisy and
dishonesty, of irresponsibility and license, a world from
which all spiritual values have been eliminated; a topsy-
turvy world in which the innocent suffers instead of the
guilty, in which the essential is subordinated to the trivial,
in which things normally recognized as evils are hailed as
real blessings; a tired world of sophisticated boredom ex-
pressing the fundamental human need for activity; a fleet-
ing world where 'the past and the future are pressing so
hard on either side that there's no room for the present

From *Studies: An Irish Quarterly Review*, LI (1962), 388-399
(Dublin: Talbot Press).

at all'; a pathetic world which 'enjoys a vicarious intimacy with death' but which nevertheless evades the reality of pain and death. Life is a vacuum in which Mr. Waugh's characters move in a vicious circle of aimlessness, boredom and futility: eternally active, they achieve nothing, their deeds being 'barely worth the attention of the most assiduous beachcomber'. Yet underneath there is 'a fatal thirst for permanence', a half articulate desire for something different and an indeterminate search for a purpose in life.

From the chaos two problems emerge as major preoccupations: Mr. Waugh is concerned first of all with the disastrous effects of Science and progress on the human personality, and, arising out of this, is his vital concern about authority or leadership in the modern world. Mr. Waugh has a horror of the Scientific Age. Under the guise of Gilbert Pinfold he confesses a hatred of 'everything in fact that had happened in his own lifetime.' The distortion normally engendered by disgust is however obviated by the honesty of the writer who combines his skill as a novelist with a power belonging properly to the historian, to interpret observed fact scientifically. No one who has read his biographical works, *Rossetti, Edmund Campion* and *Ronald Knox,* will deny Mr. Waugh's fundamental honesty, his careful scholarship and his very definite detachment.

To Mr. Waugh, the present is essentially the age in which nature is distorted, in which man is incomplete. In the world of Whispering Glades the flowers are sprayed with perfume and the droning of bees is mechanically contrived. Science supplies the deficiencies of Nature and Man, the microcosm 'equally alien from the *being* of nature and the *doing* of the machine' is reduced to 'the vile becoming'. Mr. Waugh has stated in *Robbery under Law* that man, in any age, is incomplete, being 'by nature an exile—he will never be self-sufficient or complete on this earth'. But, in so far as it is possible for man, in his earthly limitations, to become 'full' in the Renaissance ideal sense of the word, the modern world is not a propitious place in which to do so. Julia, in *Brideshead Revisited*, describes her husband, Rex Mottram, as 'something that only this ghastly age could produce. A tiny bit of a man pretending he was whole.' Rex coming from 'a harsh acquisitive world' where the only criterion of success is material, is the monstrous development of the mildly contemptible Doctor Fagan of *Decline and Fall,* for whom 'utility, economy and apparent durability are the qualities to be sought for'. Perhaps the most incisive comment on the monster modern man is to be found in the description of the state-made Miles Plastic, hero of *Love among the Ruins*: 'No clean-living, God-fearing, Victorian gentleman he; no complete man of the Renaissance; no gentile knight nor dutiful pagan nor, even noble savage—he was the Modern man'. The whole hierarchy of values which places man above the beast is quite reversed in the mind of Dame Mildred Porch who deplores the fact that children in Azania 'tried to take food from Doggies'. Man is less than sheep or goat.

Another facet of modern man's degradation is emphasized by Mr. Waugh—the loss of individuality or personal identity. Even the sexes are hardly distinguishable in the novels: "Miss Runcible wore trousers and Miles touched up his eyebrows in the dining room.' Lord Parakeet makes rude little jokes 'in a shrill emasculate voice' while Lady Circumference speaks 'in a deep bass voice' and Angela Lyne 'talked like a man'. At Margot Beste-Chetwynde's party all the guests 'wore so many different clothes of identically the same kind and spoke in the same voice—' that it was impossible for her son, Peter, to count them. Singularity is not to be tolerated in the present age. The fate of Aimee, in the *Loved One,* who is far from the standard product has the clear implication that in order to survive in the modern world one must be the standard product.

The stamp of the complete man is in his ability to lead a purposeful life. But the task of contemporary man is to 'cultivate the abhorred vacuum'. Many of the novels are concerned with man's frantic efforts to fill the void; Sebastian Flyte clinging to his teddy-bear; Tony Last surrounded by boyhood souvenirs; Ivor Claire fondling his pekinese; and Guy Crouchback, taking refuge in a dreamworld where he imagines himself 'serving the last Mass for the last Pope in a catacomb at the end of the world'. Only one complete man figures in Mr. Waugh's novels, Mr. Crouchback Senior, and he is, significantly, a classical scholar.

It would be rather absurd to suppose that Mr. Waugh is totally opposed to all science and all progress. His objection is more fundamental. He is opposed not to true science or true progress which cannot distort but to their popularized modern version: science which does not acknowledge God and progress which does not consider the ultimate end of human life. 'Man without God,' he states clearly in a review written in 1953, 'is less than man.' This is the thought underlying his appraisal of modern society.

* * *

The accusation of snobbery, so often aimed at Mr. Waugh, loses some of its force when considered in the light of his obvious preoccupation with the problem of authority in the modern world. For Mr. Waugh the aristocracy is the legitimate ruling class; consequently it is from the ranks of the decaying nobility that he often chooses his hero. Democracy is viewed in the novels as a very unstable substitute for the *ancien regime*. Mr. Outrage, 'last week's Prime Minister' of *Vile Bodies* is typical of the politicians that appear in the novels, in his remoteness from and indifference to what ought to be his main concern. It must be admitted that Mr. Waugh is extremely biased against politicians. In *Robbery Under Law,* his only overtly political work, he remarks that 'today we are plague-stricken by politics' and again 'In France and the United States it is unusual for respectable citizens to go into politics'. There is undoubted facetiousness in his attributing the dangers of the present day entirely to the political leaders, an opinion stated in the Electoral Address when he stood as candidate for the Lord Rectorship of Edinburgh University.

The public men presented in the novels are of two types, the vague older men, like Sir Samson Courteney in *Black Mischief,* who are harmlessly ineffective but retain a certain charm and the young ambitious 'go-getters' who, like Sir Humphrey of *Decline and Fall,* aspire to 'rest, rest and riches. . . .' The ineffectiveness of government by politicians is comically high-lighted in *Love among the Ruins* whose theme might be summarized as the dangerous influence of unenlightened authority on the individual and society. Mr. Waugh's condemnation of political leaders is by no means a thoughtless one. It is based on a clearly defined idea succinctly expressed in *Helena.* Analyzing a strange depression of her son, Helena states with her customary directness that the root of the problem is the possession of 'power without grace'. Her 'terrible dream of the future' centres around 'the misery of the whole world possessed of Power without Grace'.

A tripartite structure (reason: chaos: return to reason) is discernible in most of Mr. Waugh's novels but two of the early novels, *Black Mischief* and *Put Out More Flags* centered around the incorrigible Basil Seal do not fall so readily into pattern. Nor is the hero a typical Waugh hero. Basil belongs by birth to high society but he seems entirely lacking in personal integrity which was the trait common to most of the heroes. He has been so caught up in the Mayfair Jungle that the trail from his civilized origins is entirely obliterated. His very entry into the Waugh world, stopping to 'cash a bad cheque' sets the character in focus and it is consistently maintained throughout the two novels. The war which was destined to wipe out the Mayfair world drew out the best in most of Basil's contemporaries but for Basil there was no glorious call to arms but rather an unrivalled opportunity for making money. Basil is a rogue whose only positive quality seems to be his power to amuse. His position then as hero poses a problem especially when it is remembered that Mr. Waugh has expressed an affectionate interest in him. Basil is not to be dismissed as merely an amusing cad who somewhat inexplicably holds the affection of his creator.

It will be helpful at this point to examine Mr. Waugh's attitude towards his hero. The main character in a novel is generally the writer's link with the world; it is therefore a common tendency of the novelist to make the character into which he projects himself the most fascinating. This does not hold for Mr. Waugh. His leading characters with the exception of Basil Seal and Dennis Barlow (who is, in a way, a revival of Basil) are a dull lot. Paul Penny-feather's childlike simplicity is dangerously akin to culpable ignorance, Tony Last, in spite of his tragic appeal, is a bore and a prig, the pejorative 'dim' is applied at every turn to Scott-King, Guy Crouchback outdoes Tony Last in priggishness while Adam Fenwick-Symes is something of a nit-wit who allows himself to be constantly cheated. The undisciplined mob that crowds the canvas round the central dim-witted hero is, however, vastly amusing. This is an unusual scheme of things which can be attributed to the personality of Mr. Waugh—an essentially modest one—and to his ever present critical attitude of mind. Just as the stately home, the symbol of permanence in the early novels, was draughty, inconvenient and expensive to maintain, so too the characters representing the glorious past, however individual, however wise and honest and aloof are viewed in their limitations by Mr. Waugh. In their return to the world of reason two things are implied—a condemnation of the chaotic world *and* a condemnation of their failure in that world. They who were most fitted by birth and education to be the guiding lights, the stabilizing forces in a dark and restless world have not faced the challenge; they have buried their heads in the sand. The times are obviously out of joint but no one seems prepared to set things right. Does Mr. Waugh then abandon all hope of an ordered society with enlightened leadership? Activity and individuality are not enough, and personal integrity alone can be an ineffective weapon. The values of the past while superior to those of the present do not meet the challenge of the modern world. With that true artistic breadth of vision which sees beyond time Mr. Waugh realizes that two further qualities are necessary, one discernible in the character of Basil Seal, knowledge of the world, and the other which Mr. Waugh in the novel *Helena* terms grace.

* * *

The publication of *Brideshead Revisited* in 1945 caused quite a stir in literary circles. Mr. Waugh, the entertaining trifler, had suddenly emerged as a 'straight' novelist, a writer with a thesis. This new depth of seriousness confounded critics and admirers alike, and Mr. Waugh was subjected, as a result, to much adverse criticism.

The danger involved in using Catholic material for a novel was quite apparent to Mr. Waugh. As early as 1937 he had written:

It is a common complaint against Catholics that they intrude their religion into every discussion. . . . This is, in a way, true; the Catholic's life is bounded and directed by his creed at every turn and reminders of this fact may well prove tedious to his Protestant or agnostic neighbors. (*Robbery under Law*, p. 206.)

His growing moral commitment could possibly, and Mr. Sean O'Faolain suggests that it did, cost him a definite loss of power because his detachment was in jeopardy. The self-conscious technique of putting the entire narration of *Brideshead Revisited* into the mouth of Charles Ryder, a sceptical onlooker in the Catholic world of the Marchmain family, reveals in fact the effort on the part of the novelist to guard this detachment. It seems to me, however, that the attitude of those critics who see in *Brideshead Revisited* a falling-off in power can be attributed, in some measure at least, to their failure to understand the

Catholicism of Mr. Waugh. Mr. Donat O'Donnell speaks of Mr. Waugh's Catholicism as something 'hardly separable from a personal romanticism and a class loyalty . . .' (*Maria Cross* pp. 125-6) while Mr. Walter Allen states that 'for Waugh, Catholicism is a profoundly romantic thing, the core of a nostalgic dream of an ideal past by which the present is judged and found wanting'. (*The Novel Today* p. 12.) Such estimates of the Catholicism of Mr. Waugh, although to a certain extent understandable when based on *Brideshead Revisited*, are rather misleading. It is obvious from Mr. Waugh's own account of his conversion that the Church of Rome had for him no romantic or aesthetic appeal. There is an autobiographic ring in his account of Ronald Knox's conversion:

. . . he became a Catholic in violation of all his tastes and human sympathies, in obedience to his reason and in submission to what he recognized as the will of God.

Father Martin D'Arcy, S.J., 'to whom under God' Mr. Waugh owes his faith, has testified that his approach was 'factual, objective and unemotional'. An examination of the novels which followed *Brideshead Revisited* gives a more accurate notion of Mr. Waugh's Catholicism, for, in *The Loved One, Helena, Men at Arms, Officers and Gentlemen, The Ordeal of Gilbert Pinfold*, and *Unconditional Surrender* there is no trace of the self-consciousness so readily perceived in his handling of *Brideshead Revisited*.

The Catholic mind of Evelyn Waugh is already in evidence, though almost unobtrusively, in his earlier novels. It is reflected in his evident dissatisfaction with and implied condemnation of other religious sects. Mr. Prendergast of *Decline and Fall* (published two years before Mr. Waugh's conversion), a type of 'modern churchman' who 'need not commit himself to any religious belief' becomes the focus of satiric attack. He is akin to 'the priests of countless preposterous cults' later to be satirized in *The*

Loved One and he is linked in retrospect with the Oxford don who, however unwittingly, had removed the inherited axioms of Mr. Waugh's childhood faith. The violent death of Mr. Prendergast, decapitation at the hands of a maniac who considered himself the avenger of the Lord, is not at all what Mr. O'Donnell thinks it, 'the brutal murder of an inoffensive old prison chaplain'; it is Mr. Waugh's scathing condemnation of clergymen without creeds.

Mr. Waugh's opinion of the revivalist type of evangelism is clear when he allows even the frivolous society of Lady Metroland's party to recognize it as a fraud. Tony Last's religion is merely a duty he owes to the neighborhood as the local squire; it is a social act whose emptiness is quite apparent when his son is tragically killed. The two prelates of *Black Mischief* are likewise exposed to censure: the Nestorian patriarch whom no one could 'reasonably accuse of fanatical moral inflexibility' is merely a political intriguer while the Anglican bishop is a snob interested only in his personal safety. The three novels which followed *Black Mischief* (*Scoop, Work Suspended* and *Put Out More Flags*) are in no way concerned with religion; nor, strangely enough, is *Scott-King's Modern Europe* published two years after *Brideshead Revisited,* his first overtly Catholic novel.

In a country predominantly Protestant or Agnostic, the Catholic convert isolates himself from his fellows. This theme of isolation runs through the Catholic novels of Mr. Waugh, quietly expressed in *The Ordeal of Gilbert Pinfold* but much more heavily underlined in the larger canvasses of *Brideshead Revisited,* and the war novels. Catholicism replaces the more generally defined personal integrity of the hero as the isolating factor in these later novels. Mr. Waugh is not only separated from his non-Catholic friends, he is equally distant from the Catholic members of society. Of Guy Crouchback who most thoroughly represents his own attitude, he writes:

Even in his religion he felt no brotherhood . . . on the lowest as on the highest plane, there was no sympathy between him and his fellow men.

Mr. Waugh stands alone and this solitude is an asset in his profession. It enables him to guard that detachment which Mr. O'Faolain considers lost through loyalty; he can observe with equally critical eye the behaviour of his fellows whether Catholic or not.

In *Brideshead Revisited* the reader is confronted with explicit religious statement. The novel is undoubtedly self-conscious. Mr. Waugh is very much aware of his largely non-Catholic public, an awareness which leads to the technique already referred to, of presenting the story through the artistic but uncomprehending mind of the hero, Charles Ryder. In the Catholic atmosphere of the Marchmain home, Charles, a self-confessed agnostic, finds himself as some of his readers will find themselves, 'adrift on a strange sea'. *Brideshead Revisited* is the story of an aristocratic Catholic family: aristocratic and Catholic, belonging therefore to two English minorities, the one traditionally English and highly privileged, the other at once binding them with people of inferior social status and isolating them from their social equals. Critics who consider that the religion of the Marchmains is merely a colorful adornment will never understand this story. There is a conflict at the heart of the novel; a conflict experienced fully by two members of the family, Sebastian and Julia, and partially by Lord Marchmain; a conflict between their nobility and their religion. For all three, religion imposes a restraint on their liberty and each in turn rids himself of its shackles. Yet in spite of their abandonment, religion remains a disturbing agitator in the inner recesses of the mind and they are redeemed. Reconversion of the lapsed is, however, only one of two major themes.

The tripartite structure noted in the earlier novels is also discernible here. Charles emerges from what at the time seems a rational order of things into the seemingly chaotic world of the Marchmains. The difference in the structure here lies in the fact that what at first appeared unreasonable becomes the rational and Charles is converted. Instead of revulsion and rejection there is conversion. Charles' conversion and the return to the Church of Lord Marchmain, taking place as they do in the stately Marchmain home, can be seen as the apotheosis of the theme of the great country home—one of Mr. Waugh's favorite themes. After *Brideshead Revisited* the stately home is replaced by the Christian symbol of the Cross as the anchor of hope. The Cross is introduced at a climax in *Brideshead Revisited* when the dying Lord Marchmain, now inarticulate, makes the symbolic gesture. The sign brings to Charles a memory of 'the veil of the temple being rent from top to bottom' and the light of Faith dawns. In the conversion theme there is a reflection on the strange ways of God, for it is through his association with the Marchmain family, and with, in particular, the disreputable members of it, that Charles is brought to the faith. His love for Sebastian and for Julia lead to his love of God. Mr. Waugh comes close in *Brideshead Revisited,* to writing a novel in the Graham Greene manner of *The Power and the Glory* but, unlike Mr. Greene in his supposedly Catholic novels, Mr. Waugh is always careful to show his characters as reasoning beings.

There are three other members in the Marchmain family: the overzealous and pious mother, a fanatical and somewhat uncompromising elder son, Lord Brideshead, and Cordelia, the only happy person in the family. What is significant from the Catholic point of view is that, however estranged one section of the family becomes from the other, however far the one strays from Catholic roots, they have all one characteristic in common—an impressive conviction of the truth of their religion. 'Is it nonsense?' asks Sebastian of Charles, 'I wish it were. It sometimes sounds terribly sensible to me.' Julia, in reply to Charles's '. . . you do know at heart that it's all bosh, don't you?' says simply 'How I wish it were.' Behind the conviction of his characters is Mr. Waugh's own testimony of the truth of the Catholic claims which may be temporarily ignored and rejected but not permanently denied. *Brideshead Revisited* succeeds in conveying the tremendous power of Catholicism in the lives of its adherents, a power which is due, not to mystical or superstitious forces, but to the shattering truth of its claims.

It might well be asked why Mr. Waugh thought it necessary to create Charles Ryder as a definite link with his public, or whether having created him, the exclamations of irritation expressed in such phrases as 'mumbo jumbo' and 'bosh' will find an echo in the non-Catholic reader's heart? The attitude of non-Catholic England towards Catholicism has changed radically since the Second World War. Emphasis is now laid on similarities between the Roman Church and other Christian denominations. *Brideshead Revisited* was written before the close of the war and it must be examined in the light of pre-war facts. Hilaire Belloc writing in 1937 states:

The decline in religious belief, the growth of scepticism and indifference have in no way affected as yet . . . the Protestant character of England . . . the essential feeling of hostility against Rome and all the Catholic culture of Europe is as strong as ever ('An Essay on the Nature of Contemporary England').

If this be true, then the statement throws some light on Mr. Waugh's rather timid handling of his Catholic material in *Brideshead Revisited*.

* * *

The symbol of the Cross noted as the emerging anchor symbol in *Brideshead Revisited* becomes the major theme in *The Loved One*. It is naive to dismiss this novel as a biting satire on California burial customs, another of Mr. Waugh's cruel jokes. In fact *The Loved One* is a study of modern man's sentimental attitude towards death. Under the satire is a plea for the old-fashioned but sane attitude to life and death, for a re-appraisal of the Role of the Cross, the center of Christian symbolism. Mr. O'Donnell accuses *The Loved One* of invading 'forbidden places—the mortuary and the cemetery—in a spirit of atrocious levity'. This can be substantiated but it is not the whole truth. The artistic mind of Mr. Waugh was undoubtedly attracted by the very original material of Forest Lawn but, and this is at least equally important, his Catholic mind was shocked by the travesty of death in the daily routine of Forest Lawn.

In an article entitled 'Half in Love with Easeful Death' written for *The Tablet,* Mr. Waugh gives the real key to the understanding of *The Loved One.* Replying to Mr. Bruce Barton who had claimed that the symbols used at Forest Lawn breathed life and hope in contrast with the hopelessness of the traditional Cross symbol, Mr. Waugh states: 'The Christian visitor might here remark that by far the commonest feature of other graveyards is still the Cross, a symbol in which previous generations have found more Life and Hope than in the most elaborately watered shrub.' The ideal of Forest Lawn is 'to shade off . . . the moment of transition' from life to death. Forest Lawn consciously turns its back on the reality of death on the 'grim traditional alternatives of Heaven and Hell'; it promises 'immediate eternal happiness to all its inmates . . . we are very far here from traditional conception of an adult soul naked at the judgment seat and a body turning to corruption'. The external beauty, serenity and hope which Whispering Glades, the Forest Lawn of *The Loved One,* shows the world is symptomatic of man's fear of death, of his flight from painful experience, of his childish wishful thinking. The Loved One is not a soul whose preparedness to meet its Creator is the important thing; he is simply a body to be dressed elegantly for his journey to guaranteed bliss. The passport to eternal happiness is a substantial fee. Here the sentimental irreligious attitude of the Dreamer is exposed as was the revivalist religion of Mrs. Ape in *Vile Bodies* as commercial exploitation of the

45

gullible. In upholding the dignity of death Mr. Waugh is emphasizing the dignity of man. Suffering, pain and death are bitter pills in an era whose chief concern is material progress and comfortable living, and these are the pills which Mr. Waugh prescribes in *The Loved One.*

Helena, the novel which followed *The Loved One,* is based on the few known facts of the life of Saint Helena who discovered the True Cross. Mr. Waugh states the theme in a short work entitled *The Holy Places* published in a limited edition in 1952. Helena's task was: 'to turn the eyes of the world back to the planks of wood on which . . . salvation hung'. Helena was raised up to assert 'in sensational form, a dogma that was in danger of neglect', that God became man. The closing lines of the novel express Mr. Waugh's belief in the value of the Cross:

> But the wood has endured. . . . For it states a fact.
> Hounds are checked, hunting wild. A horn calls clear
>   through the covert.
> Helena casts them back on the scent.
> Above all the babble of her age and ours, she makes one
>   blunt assertion.
> And there alone lies hope.

*　　*　　*

What strikes the reader of Mr. Waugh's Catholic novels is the strength of his faith and his quiet, resigned, one might almost call it, his joyless acceptance of all it entails. Catholicism involves sacrifice but because it gives life a meaning the sacrifice is worthwhile. The Faith gives him daily life and for it he abandons as Edmund Campion had done 'all smaller loyalties and affections'.

The Faith as a way of life is the core of the war novels. Like the Marchmains of *Brideshead Revisited,* Guy Crouchback and his father are aristocratic Catholics, but for them there is no wavering from the straight and narrow road prescribed by their religion. Guy is more than the romantic hero dispossessed, living in political and spiritual isolation. He is the professional Catholic whose approach to serious problems is that of the highly educated and intellectual Catholic. As such he reflects Mr. Waugh's rational approach to religion. *Men At Arms* is a very fine novel and this in spite of the fact that it is concerned largely with dry theological issues. For Guy there are two major problems, the morality of war and the private domestic problem which gives rise to dispassionate speculation on the theological attitude towards resuming marital relations with the wife who had divorced him. His intellectual Catholic mind is further emphasized in his choice of a friend—he chooses Ivor Claire, detecting a remote kinship with him, a common aloofness '. . . each in his own way saw life *sub specie aeternitatis* . . .'—and by his various references to the reality of the supernatural. Guy not only reflects Mr. Waugh's rational appreciation of Catholicism, he is also the embodiment of his creator's joyless acceptance of the Faith and a symbol of his great solitude.

Adequate treatment of the character of Mr. Crouchback, senior, is not possible within the confines of this study. From the Catholic point of view he is a figure of paramount importance in Mr. Waugh's novel-world for he expresses the simple grace of Catholic living. "He is a 'just man'; not particularly judicious, not at all judicial, but 'just' in the full sense of the psalmist. . . ." Mr. Crouchback is a foil to Guy whose 'few dry grains of faith' contrast sharply with the warm strength of his father's belief. He too is a man dispossessed. His ancestral home, a large part of his inheritance, his beloved wife, all are lost to him. Yet his reaction has nothing in common with the ruined squire 'of Victorian iconography'. Guy and his father are equally punctilious in religious observance but Guy's religion has something of the mere routine of Tony Last and the stern uncompromising attitude of Lord Brideshead. Guy, dispossessed, existed in a joyless vacuum, isolated, but Mr. Crouchback had a natural advantage over him, being fortified by a memory 'which kept only the good things and rejected the ill'. Guy's character is evolving; he is travelling towards a point where his father has happily arrived. His remarriage with Virginia in the final volume of the trilogy, the first 'positively unselfish action' in his life, is a step in this direction. It is tempting to suggest that Mr. Waugh is also travelling towards this point but it would be perhaps more realistic to say that while Mr. Waugh's acceptance of the Faith seems joyless he recognizes through the character of Mr. Crouchback that it need not necessarily be so.

Mr. Crouchback fulfills a function akin to but transcending that of Basil Seal in the earlier novels. Basil differed from his contemporaries in an ability to come to terms with his world—a power deriving from astute knowledge of that world. Mr. Crouchback, too, is at home in his world. Catholicism is no obstacle to his intercourse with others. His 'steadfast benevolence' endears him to all the residents of the Marine Hotel; he is 'the symbol of their security'. In a word, the figure of Guy's father is for Mr. Waugh the complete man. Scholar, gentleman and Catholic, he is the ideal whom every man should wish to be.

Catholicism, then, in Mr. Waugh's novels emerges as a coherent philosophy whose claims, however shattering, are based on truth and are therefore acceptable to the intellect. It is a religion of death and suffering, not 'dark and defeatist', as Mr. O'Donnell suggests but rather as Saint John of the Cross has put it, a religion in which 'the endurance of darkness is preparation for great light'. The Faith is the dawning of light for Charles Ryder, the great motivating force that impels Helena to her tremendous discovery, the illuminating factor in Guy Crouchback's life which resigns him to the reversal of fortune and for Mr. Crouchback, it is the source of immeasurable joy. The Faith is the eternal kaleidoscope shaking into pattern the crazy outlines of a chaotic world. Mr. Waugh has found what Mr. Kenneth Pearson has very aptly called 'a cast-iron philosophy' in the cumulative wisdom of the Catholic Church. This philosophy will be a determining factor in preventing the dust of oblivion from settling on his pages.

D. J. Dooley

•

THE STRATEGY OF THE CATHOLIC NOVELIST

In his article "The Catholic Novelist in the U.S.A." (*Catholic World*, February, 1959), Stephen P. Ryan raises some interesting questions about the approach of contemporary Catholic novelists to their material. He expresses his amazement that "Catholicism and the Catholic way of life emerge in the hands of contemporary Catholic writers as almost totally grim and forbidding," and he wonders why some of them do not portray the Church in a more favorable light.

Part of the answer is that depravity is easier to depict than sanctity; another part is that the novelist must consider the nature of the world he is writing about. It seems to me that the Catholic novelist will succeed best if he tries to shock people into an awareness of how chaotic their society has become because it has forgotten spiritual values, or if he shows the presence of grace where it is most unexpected. The former is the characteristic method of Waugh, the latter of Greene.

The writer must be true to his material, but he must also communicate his thoughts to a particular audience. The contemporary reading public likes strong stuff. George Orwell's essay "Raffles and Miss Blandish" provides some evidence for this—if evidence is needed. Turning to a book written in 1939 after discussing a book written in 1900, he comments, "Now for a header into the cesspool." Torture, murder, and sexual perversions are almost taken for granted in James Hadley Chase's *No Or-*

From *Catholic World*, CLXXXIX (July, 1959), 300-304. Reprinted by permission of the author and the publisher.

chids for Miss Blandish; the weak are the victims of the strong, and moral considerations are irrelevant. Orwell goes on to point out that much more important novelists than Chase use the same spicy ingredients and manifest the same disregard for moral imperatives; in fact he says that, though the common people may still be living in the world of absolute good and evil, the intellectuals have long since escaped it. If Orwell is correct, the present-day audience is not prepared for holiness.

It is a commonplace that many of us have to make a special effort to acquire the proper perspective from which we can appreciate the classics of the past. *Paradise Lost* is a case in point. C. S. Lewis felt it necessary to write a book-length "Preface" telling readers how to approach the poem; and Douglas Bush came near to losing his temper over contemporary misunderstandings of it: "It is not altogether (Milton's) fault if readers debauched by sentimental and romantic liberalism and naturalism are incapable of either intellectual or emotional response to the classical Christian, medieval, and Renaissance doctrines of law and order in the soul, in society, and in the cosmos."

If the modern world has little sympathy for Milton, even though it regards him as an apostle of liberty, a defender of freedom of speech and of the press, what sympathy is it likely to have for an attitude of life which reminds it of the Inquisition? The famous historian Carl Becker described the present climate of opinion as one in which "it is quite impossible for us to regard man as the child of God for whom the earth was created as a temporary habitation." In so troubled a climate, the pious tale will appeal only to the already converted; other readers will put it aside as "out-dated" or "oversimplified" or (most damning adjective of all) "sentimental."

The career of Evelyn Waugh offers an object lesson in what a writer must not do if he is to avoid being damned by the reviewers and the non-Catholic reading public as a teller of pious tales. Though he was converted to Catholicism as early as 1930, and though he wrote a life of the

Jesuit martyr Edmund Campion in 1935, Catholicism does not seem to have been an informing principle in his early novels. He used his mordant wit to show the other side of the coin—the disorder of a world from which religion was missing. Even here Peter Quennell spotted "intervals of solemnity, when the satirist gave way to the Catholic moralist . . ."; but *Decline and Fall, Vile Bodies,* and *Black Mischief* were generally regarded as light-hearted satires. *A Handful of Dust,* however, could not be read as an amusing comedy; it was as soul-searching as the poem from which it derived its title, Eliot's *Waste Land.* This is perhaps Waugh's most successful novel; though it did not gain him a large following, it brought him critical attention; and it did so by showing in a disturbing way how a society crumbles when faith is gone from it.

At this time Waugh was gaining increasing recognition as a novelist whose development was worth watching. Edmund Wilson put his stamp of approval on him in a survey of his novels which appeared in the *New Yorker* in 1944—" 'Never Apologize, Never Explain': The Art of Evelyn Waugh." He called Waugh the only first-rate comic genius to appear in English since Shaw, and praised *A Handful of Dust* as a masterpiece—Waugh was remarkably successful in conveying "the impression of a terror, of a feeling that the bottom is just about to drop out of things. . . ." Though he had no great regard for Waugh's political and religious beliefs, Wilson had great respect for him as an artist: "Evelyn Waugh is today a declared Tory and a Roman Catholic convert; he believes in the permanence of the social classes and, presumably, in the permanence of evil. . . . But . . . he does not set up as a guide; and his opinions do not damage his fiction. About this fiction there is nothing schematic and nothing doctrinaire . . . everything in it has grown out of experience and everything has emotional value."

But, alas, disillusionment came swiftly; in January of 1946, Wilson wrote, "The new novel by Evelyn Waugh— *Brideshead Revisited*—has been a bitter blow to this critic." For some things in it, especially the early chapters, he had high praise; but in the end he described it as a "Catholic tract." Yet he found it impossible to believe that the author had conveyed any genuine religious feeling; Catholicism in *Brideshead* seemed "more like an exorcistic rite than a force of regeneration." Wilson felt that Waugh put more genuine feeling into his snobbish veneration of the upper class: "his cult of the high nobility is allowed to become so rapturous and solemn that it finally gives the impression of being the only real religion in the book." He predicted cynically that its sentimentality would assure it a high place in the best-seller lists.

Thus Waugh lost one of his greatest admirers. In his subsequent reviews of Waugh's books, Wilson has not been able to overcome his feeling of disillusionment or to conceal his distaste for the religion which, in his opinion, vitiates Waugh's art. Discussing a reprint of *Edmund Campion,* he wrote, "If we had no source but Mr. Waugh, we might assume that the Society of Jesus had always consisted solely of mild spirited servants of God, who had never had anything to do with rigging racks or lighting fagots of their enemies." Similarly he found it hard to praise *The Loved One,* even though he regarded it as a return to Waugh's earlier manner; after some rather petty fault-finding, he wrote a brief essay on the cowardice of Catholics in refusing to admit that death is the end of our existence. Thus we see that an overt statement of belief produces a reaction against itself; when Waugh brought Catholicism into his novels as a positive force, he alienated a very influential critic and provoked attacks, not just against his novels, but also against his religion itself.

Similarly R. B. Heilman, in discussing *Brideshead,* moved on from the faults of the novel to the faults of the religion which inspired it or at least the inhibitions it imposes on the novelist. His article began with a comparison between *Brideshead* and Thomas Hardy's *Jude the Obscure,* in which there is a character named Sue Bridehead. The basic contrast, of course, is a religious one. To Waugh, "religion is a value, a forming impulse which takes precedence over all others, not a set of ethical regulations. . . ." This point of view, Heilman said, would have seemed fantastic to Victorian novel-readers; it recommends a return to a way of life which to Hardy seemed fossilized. Nor is it "the characteristic way out of the twentieth century, which has pretty thoroughly damned Waugh but is, ironically, quite hospitable to the once-public enemy, Hardy." Like Edmund Wilson, Heilman complained that Waugh's religion interferes with his art; it prevents him from understanding or imagining the psychology of unbelievers. He asked the question "whether identification with a religious institution brings about a total adjustment which dims the novelist's imagination of kinds of experience upon which, nevertheless, he must as novelist draw." A state of tension is the proper condition for creation: "That condition is hardly the peace that passeth understanding, but rather the not wholly achieved allegiance, the felt resistance that extends comprehension, the dissonances and intractabilities . . . that intrude upon quieting finalities."

It would be easy to multiply evidence that, since *Brideshead,* Waugh's critics have looked at his books in a different way. We might cite as examples a rather juvenile survey of his novels by D. S. Savage, and two much more mature ones by Joan Griffiths and Rose Macaulay—all of which have the same theme, the harm which Waugh's religious principles have done to his books. Consequently the serious reading public finds it difficult to approach Waugh without unfavorable preconceptions. Reviewing *The Ordeal of Gilbert Pinfold* in the *New York Times,* Gerald Sykes called Waugh "perhaps the best polemicist of our day. As his novelistic powers have suffered a decline and fall, his capacity to chop down his enemies has become, by compensation, truly impressive." Thus he was blinded by prejudice from appreciating a novel which, to the more discriminating English reviewers, seemed an indication of Waugh's astonishing virtuosity. Reviewing Frederick J. Stopp's book on Waugh, the *New Yorker* referred to the "increasingly smug and parochial religiosity" of his works. As we look at Waugh's recent themes—Hollywood mortuary establishments in *The Loved One*, the finding of the Cross in *Helena*, the Second World War in *Men at Arms* and *Officers and Gentlemen*, the welfare state in *Love Among the Ruins*, psychological self-portraiture in *The Ordeal of Gilbert Pinfold*—we see no such increase of religiosity; but the *New Yorker* reviewer is blinded by *Brideshead*. It is to be feared that the same is true of a large part of Waugh's potential audience.

In a review of E. E. Hales' *The Catholic Church in the Modern World*, the *Times Literary Supplement* recently commented on the strong antagonism which has often been shown to the Church: "The fact remains that the Roman Catholic Church seems to attract extremes of love or hate that, in the end, can only be referred to the tremendous claims she makes." Given the existence of such antagonism, the novelist who wishes to make an impact on the modern world will have to suit his strategy to it. I am not suggesting that he should pander to the taste for sensationalism; but he must at least consider what subjects and what approaches to them his audience is not prepared to understand. As Wilson's approval of Waugh's earlier books shows, the fact that a writer is a Catholic does not mean automatic and prejudiced condemnation of his books. He can even find acceptance for Catholic themes, provided his presentation of them is subtle and convincing. Perhaps the key is to be found in Heilman's discussion of *Brideshead*: the modern world finds it difficult to sympathize with the settled state of belief, the quieting finality; it is more in harmony with and more interested in the state of tension. Consequently if the novelist deals with sanctity he is most likely to gain acceptance if he shows, as J. F. Powers does so well in his short stories, the temptations that afflict it. If he tries to portray the Church as a haven or refuge, a shelter from the modern world, he cannot expect to find the modern world agreeing with him.

Marston LaFrance

CONTEXT AND STRUCTURE OF

EVEYLN WAUGH'S *BRIDESHEAD REVISITED*

Brideshead Revisited, which appeared in 1945, seems to have provided both the impetus and focal point for most of the existing criticism of Evelyn Waugh's fiction. If one wishes to discuss the six eariler "comic" novels—*Decline and Fall* (1928), *Vile Bodies* (1930), *Black Mischief* (1932), *A Handful of Dust* (1934), *Scoop* (1938), and *Put Out More Flags* (1942)—it has become more or less customary to mention how *Brideshead Revisited,* the seventh novel and the first "serious" work, differs from them. And if one examines Mr. Waugh's post-war novels, *Brideshead Revisited* can always be used as a kind of norm: a later novel belongs either with the serious works, or with the peculiar comic tradition established by the first six novels. However, *Brideshead Revisited* has itself evoked sufficient critical disagreement to imply that, even at this late date, it still presents problems worth investigating.

One of the difficulties confronting the student of Mr. Waugh's fiction is the virtual impossibility of placing this author securely within a single comic tradition. His obviously comic novels seem far too meaningful to be regarded as mere caricature, and yet they lack both the tinge of bitterness one normally associates with irony, and the moral indignation which usually accompanies satire. Erwin Stürzl identifies him with the tradition of Defoe and Smol-

From *Twentieth Century Literature*, X (April, 1964), 12-18. Reprinted by permission of author and publisher.

lett;[1] and while this is certainly debatable, it emphasizes the importance of plot and craftsmanship in the creation of the earlier novels. The distinctions usually accorded Mr. Waugh are that, until 1945, his fiction reveals a steady progression away from this craftsman's tradition and toward the more conventional novel in which action grows out of motivation firmly grounded upon character, and that *Brideshead Revisited* represents a complete escape from his earlier tradition. Although critics have disagreed with both of these judgments, none has examined *Brideshead Revisited* within the specific context provided by the six novels which preceded it, a context of both thought and technique. Such a consideration will reveal a remarkable amount of similarity between this novel and the earlier ones; further a detailed examination of these similarities will expose what is perhaps a basic structural flaw in *Brideshead Revisited*.

One might well begin with Brideshead Castle itself. By 1945 no reader of Mr. Waugh's fiction should have been surprised at finding yet another great house in the novel. King's Thursday, Anchorage House, Doubting Hall, Hetton Abbey, Boot Magna, Malfrey—all of Mr. Waugh's great houses represent the stability of England's past when the national life was under the control of a responsible aristocracy. All of these houses are in decline, whether from outright destruction (King's Thursday) or a gradual decay of the family line (Doubting Hall, Hetton, Brideshead), and their decline functions as a sort of graph of the aristocracy's increasing irresponsibility and loss of power. The role of Brideshead does not depart from the established pattern; at the close of the novel the Flyte family is completely dispersed, the elder son disinherited, and the house and grounds are being defaced by the army.

Like the great house itself, the characters of *Brideshead Revisited* are indigenous to the world created by the earlier novels. Anthony Blanche is closely related to Ambrose Silk of *Put Out More Flags*: both are esthetes, homosexuals, wanderers without any sense of nationality, and both characters are given the responsibility of passing aesthetic judgment in their respective novels. Ambrose Silk states that "European culture has become conventual; we must make it coenobitic," an end which the action of the remainder of *Put Out More Flags* pursues; Anthony Blanche both warns Ryder about becoming involved with the Flyte family, and offers the only judgment upon his Latin-American paintings which Ryder accepts. Rex Mottram is Mr. Waugh's self-seeking man of affairs, a social and moral buccaneer whom the reader has already encountered in Basil Seal (*Black Mischief, Put Out More Flags*) and, to a lesser extent, in Jock Grant-Menzies (*A Handful of Dust*). He is the "coarse-grained knight-robber of worldly success" to whom Mr. Waugh's "passive, rather melancholy and isolated central figure" usually loses the girl. [2] Rex has neither the social aplomb of Jock Grant-Menzies nor the sense of humor of Basil Seal, but he is endowed with a ruthlessness which, if he were successful, would eventually permit him to become another Lord Copper (*Scoop*). Mr. Samgrass is cut from the same bolt of cloth as Philbrick (*Decline and Fall*) and Youkoumian (*Black Mischief*); all three characters are distinguished by a lack of any personal moral center, and by a remarkable facility to adapt profitably to any given circumstances in which they are able to involve themselves.

Sebastian Flyte has much in common with Sir Alistair Digby-Vaine-Trumpington (*Decline and Fall*). Both are charming, wealthy, and extremely casual Oxford undergraduates from the aristocracy. Sir Alistair is to Paul Pennyfeather as Sebastian is to Charles Ryder—the emissary, "half satyr, half messenger of the gods," from an unfamiliar world to an innocent but interested outsider (Stopp, 65). Sebastian degenerates into alcoholism and homosexuality, while Sir Alistair, after drinking his way from *Decline and Fall* to *Put Out More Flags,* finally redeems himself by joining the army as an enlisted man, volunteering for hazardous duty, and making his wife pregnant; otherwise there is little distinction between them.

Charles Ryder is Mr. Waugh's familiar protagonist who descends from Paul Pennyfeather and Adam Fenwick-Symes (*Vile Bodies*) through Tony Last (*A Handful of Dust*), William Boot (*Scoop*), and Cedric Lyne (*Put Out More Flags*). These are the "passive, rather melancholy and isolated" central figures, dilettantes, innocents to the world into which they are thrust, less actively protagonists than characters acted upon. "Just as the author is the implicit mainspring of his world . . . so the innocent hero is the concealed fulcrum of the action" (Stopp, 197). According to F. J. Stopp, these heroes tend to develop in either of two directions:

The jungle of the world forces the innocent hero to become either an exploiter or a victim of surrounding chaos, a cad, or a dullard, though still not properly a moral agent. To put it simply, Paul Pennyfeather has the choice of graduating through the intermediate stage of John Beaver (*A Handful of Dust*) to the fully developed bounder in Basil Seal (or Rex Mottram); or through the stage of Adam Fenwick-Symes to the matured victim in Tony Last (or Cedric Lyne). (Stopp, 199.)

And both directions are seen in Charles Ryder. He is the bounder toward his wife and toward Rex Mottram, but he ends the novel as the victim: "I never built anything, and I forfeited the right to watch my son grow up. I'm homeless, childless, middle-aged, loveless." [3]

Mr. Waugh's female characters divide into two groups; Stopp calls one group the waifs, and the other might well be called the bosses. Julia and Cordelia Flyte are waifs in the direct line of Brenda Last crumpled before the fire with her bread and milk, Agatha Runcible (*Vile Bodies*) hopelessly drunk and trying to drive a racing car, Kätchen coaxing money out of William Boot, and Barbara Sothill (*Put Out More Flags*) desperately trying to assign the terrible Connolly children to a billet. Lady Marchmain is a boss in the tradition of Margot Metroland (*Decline and Fall*)—though without Margot's whimsical amorality—Lady Seal, and Julia Stitch (*Scoop*) — though without

Julia's sense of humor. However, Erwin Stürzl states that, whether they are waifs or bosses,

Der Satiriker Waugh stellt die Mehrzahl seiner weiblichen Charaktere als kalte, herzlose Wesen dar, die sich auf die Anbahnung von Liebesbeziehungen wohl verstehen, as jedoch mit dem Eherersprechen nicht sehr genau nehmen und jederzeit ihre materiellen Interessen in kühler Berechnung zu wahren wissen. Nicht selten verursachen sie so, wie etwa Brenda Last, . . . den Ruin ja gänzlichen Untergang jenes Mannes, mit dem sie in Berührung kommen (Stürzl, 318.)

This judgment applies to both Lady Marchmain and Julia if one substitutes religion for "material interests" as the determining force behind their actions.

Brideshead Revisited also reveals the eccentric father, a figure seen at his best, perhaps, in Colonel Blount of Doubting Hall (*Vile Bodies*). Sebastian and Julia again reveal the strange brother and sister relationship, half affection, half hostility, encountered earlier in Basil Seal and Barbara Sothill. And in all of Mr. Waugh's first seven novels the innocent hero becomes involved in the brave new world through the merest chance. Paul Pennyfeather is expelled from Oxford as a result of the Bollinger Club dinner in which he did not participate; Adam Fenwick-Symes has his autobiography destroyed as obscene literature by customs officials; Basil Seal, at the time when the situation in Azania becomes pregnant with possibility, just happens to need a fresh means of escape from the machinations of his mother; William Boot is sent to Ishmaelia as a consequence of mistaken identity; and Ryder becomes involved with the Flyte family because Sebastian happens to vomit in through the open window of his room.

Finally, before moving on to examine more important aspects of *Brideshead Revisited,* it should be noted that the well-known Proustian passage at the beginning of "A Twitch upon the Thread" apparently harks back to a device Mr. Waugh used earlier at least twice. This passage is given to Ryder, the narrator, but in no other section of the novel is he allowed so sustained a flight in such a style of language; moreover, the function of this passage is to provide an aesthetic statement which seems to apply more to the novel as a whole than to Ryder alone. The use of such a device is obvious in *Decline and Fall;* all action stops, and the author himself comes on stage.

For an evening at least the shadow that has flitted about this narrative under the name of Paul Pennyfeather materialized into the solid figure of an intelligent, well-educated, well-conducted young man. [4]

In *Vile Bodies* a comparable statement is given to Mr. Outrage, and as with Ryder, both the language and the significance of the statement to the novel as a whole seem to transcend the capabilities assigned to this character.

They (the post-war generation) had a chance after the war that no generation has ever had. There was a whole civilization to be saved and remade—and all they seem to do is play the fool. [5]

In all three instances the author apparently drops the mask for a moment to speak directly to the reader.

II

If Mr. Waugh's first seven novels reveal a progression away from the comic and toward the conventional, this progression cannot be a very steady one. Basil Seal's adventures with the frightful Connolly children in *Put Out More Flags,* for example, are as hilariously comic as anything in *Decline and Fall.* On the other hand, the first serious attempt at what may be called a conventional characterization is probably Tony Last in *A Handful of Dust,* but no other character in Mr. Waugh's fiction before the first part of *Brideshead Revisited* seems more completely realized or invested with a greater depth than this one is. Also, aside from the similarities already mentioned, there is quite a bit more evidence against considering *Brideshead Revisited* a complete escape from the earlier tradition.

The general structure of this novel is the same as that of the earlier works: an innocent hero is introduced, through an emissary, by mere chance, into a strange environment which acts upon him to the extent of making him either an exploiter or a victim of this environment. And within this general structure several lesser episodes are analogous to aspects of the earlier novels. The two scenes in which Rex Mottram and his cronies talk at Brideshead seem to be solidly within the comic tradition. The wonderful fencing matches between Ryder and his father cannot lag far behind Mottram's conversations. The excellent scene in which Ryder frustrates Lady Marchmain's careful plot to keep Sebastian sober should recall Basil Seal's ability to frustrate his mother's plots for his welfare. Lady Marchmain is—presumably—made a sympathetic character largely through the only significant speech that Cara is allowed in the entire novel (102-103); and this device again should recall an old trick of Mr. Waugh, the craftsman, who makes the reader see an important character through the eyes of Brenda's friends. If it is less obvious when Basil Seal is seen through the eyes of his mother, sister, or mistress, it is also less successful, for Basil is by no means as bad as critics have supposed him to be. (He has intelligence, courage, a superb sense of humor, and he seems actively aware of the threats hidden in modernism and progress; also, like all charming rogues, he is much more interested in the game itself than in the ends which result.) [6] Mr. Waugh, due to the demands imposed by comedy upon dramatic necessity, developed a habit of killing off his characters in the comic novels: Little Lord Tangent, Prendergast (*Decline and Fall*); Florrie, Balcairn, Agatha (*Vile Bodies*); Prudence, the Pretender, Seth (*Black Mischief*); John Andrew, Dr. Messinger, Tony Last—whose fate is more horrible than death itself (*A Handful of Dust*); Cedric

Lyne (*Put Out More Flags*). This habit reveals itself more humanely in *Brideshead Revisited* through the removal of Sebastian; the "forerunner" must necessarily disappear in order to leave the field of Ryder open to Julia.

Perhaps an even stronger argument against Mr. Waugh's escape from the earlier tradition lies in the difference between the two main parts of *Brideshead Revisited*. In "Et in Arcadia Ego" the dramatic force of the clash of will between Sebastian and his mother is strong enough to sustain a style which now and again deteriorates into an intrusive obviousness in "A Twitch upon the Thread." What seems to be the principal rhetorical device used—a self-consciously poetic padding—is easily illustrated in a brief passage from the second section.

I saw her to bed; the *blue* lids fell *over her eyes;* her *pale* lips moved *on the pillow,* but whether to wish me good-night or to murmur a prayer—*a jingle of the nursery that came to her now in the twilit world between sorrow and sleep; some ancient pious rhyme that had come down to Nanny Hawkins from centuries of bedtime whispering, through all the changes of language, from the days of pack-horses on the Pilgrim's Way—* I did not know. (292-293; my italics.)

The italicized words add very little that is material to the action; the action has to stop while they are read. Their tone of poetic lushness becomes somewhat cloying when it is not informed by the authority of satire or irony, as it is when William Boot writes such passages for his "Lush Places" column. In short, the dramatic motivation is so strong in the first section that the characters present the pleasant illusion of taking control of the story; while religion, the force which determines and directs the action, is obviously present, both it and the presence of the author are eclipsed by the immediacy of Sebastian's conflict with his family. But in the second part this immediacy seems to disappear with Sebastian. The author, armed with the determining force of religion, emerges to reveal his superb comic craftsmanship taking control of what is meant to be a serious situation. Hence, both dramatic motivation and character are forced to give way in the direction of the pasteboard puppets of the earlier tradition.

Hence, Stephen Spender is correct in stating that "the lack of sense of moral proportion in *Brideshead Revisited* is probably artistic rather than religious. It comes from trying to state comic seriousness . . . as didactic moralizing, and the absurd as sober truth." [7] To draw this distinction between an artistic and a religious failure, one need only consider Cordelia's tale of Sebastian (303-309). Sebastian, in Cordelia's words, "maimed as he is— no dignity, no power of will," has presumably at the nadir of his degradation found God. From the point of view of religion one sees the fact and dismisses the process. But from the point of view of the novelist's art the process all but obliterates the fact. The reader has become so committed to Sebastian in the first part of the novel, and the progressive degeneration is described so vividly, that one cannot but feel an almost tragic sense of waste in Sebastian as all hope for his recovery has to be abandoned. Then, when Cordelia states that he has achieved holiness —"Oh yes, Charles, that's what you've got to understand about Sebastian"—and that people in his condition "are very near and dear to God," one's aesthetic sense rebels, even though one can—intellectually—understand the religious justification.

By the same token, the latter part of the novel reveals several actions which seem artistically out of place in a conventionally realistic novel, while they would be entirely acceptable in the earlier comic tradition. Ryder has married Boy Mulcaster's sister, but the intelligence attributed earlier to Ryder should have led him to avoid such a woman. Ryder, after two years abroad, has no desire whatsoever to see his own children, the daughter he has never seen and the son for whom he later is made to reveal a great yearning (and he reveals it to Hooper, of all people). Ryder practices the chess-game morality of the comic tradition: because Celia has been unfaithful to him he believes himself released from the responsibilities of a husband and a father. Julia follows the same pattern: "she is bad, and if she gives up the one thing she wants most—it happens to be Charles—possibly God will forgive her for her other sins." [8] Charles and Julia move into Brideshead and the arrangement is blandly accepted by all concerned, just as it would be in the world of *Vile Bodies*. Bridey, with his matchbox collection, his wooden dogmatism, and his Mrs. Muspratt, seems entirely a creation of Mr. Waugh's best comic craftsmanship. Ryder's objection to Father Mackay—in itself questionable due to Ryder's casual connection with the family—is emphasized, for purposes of contrast, at the expense of characterization; in a delicate situation he is given the speech of a lout—" 'Mumbo-jumbo is off,' I said, 'the witch-doctor has gone' " (327). Then, after his absurd last-ditch fight, Ryder suddenly falls on his knees and prays for a sign from Lord Marchmain. And Lord Marchmain, after twenty-five years apart from the church, after his earlier curt dismissal of the priest, obliges. In view of Mr. Waugh's six previous novels, it seems reasonable to assume that, artistically, the expert comic craftsman has once again produced a tidy finale from the satiric rag and bone shop of his own heart, and has mutilated his puppets until they conformed to it.

III

It is important to realize that in *Brideshead Revisited*, religion is the ultimate force behind the actions of the inhabitants of the world into which the hero is thrust. This structural element is probably the basis for most of the critical squabbles which have arisen over this novel. F. J. Stopp states correctly that "the world of Mr. Waugh's novels is a fantasy world, but with moral implications. . . . While the general implications are moral, the specific fates meted out to the characters are governed by the element of fantasy" (193). In each of the earlier novels there is also a determining force behind the action of the characters in this fantasy world. This force may be greed, irresponsible self-satisfaction, getting a newspaper scoop whether true or false. The point to be stressed is that all of these forces, determining action in the world of comic fantasy, are in themselves to be condemned. This implicit condemnation of the force or value behind the action is what makes Mr. Waugh's comedy satiric.

In *Brideshead Revisited*, however, one finds the same function being discharged by a force which, in itself, is obviously not to be condemned. If, at the same time, the comic world of fantasy had been exchanged for the conventional realistic frame of reference, this change in the quality of the determining force would not have caused any difficulty; some such force must lie behind the action in any novel, but the operation of such a force in the realistic novel is governed by the demands of dramatic motivation and character, not by the author's ability to manipulate the situations of a plot. This whole essay, however, has argued that in *Brideshead Revisited* the fantasy world has not been done away with. Thus, the real issue presented by this novel is, again, not the religion in itself, but the confusion which must inevitably result when an highly desirable force is used to determine action in a world which is still fundamentally one of comic fantasy. For if this structural flaw is allowed to creep into a novel, the reader is confronted with a dilemma: he must either accept the fantasy world by rejecting the determining force behind it—as is normally done with the comic novels—or, if he wishes to accept the determining force, he finds himself aesthetically obligated to reject the implication that such a force can operate only in a world of fantasy. According to A. J. Neame, at least one Catholic reader felt compelled to choose the first alternative: "one of Isabel Clarke's cousins who was not in the know mistook [*Brideshead Revisited*] for an anti-Catholic tract, and imagined that Mr. Waugh had only found the Faith later." [9] Such a reading may indeed seem incredible, but it represents the logical extreme of the result which follows from the structural flaw described above.

Placing *Brideshead Revisited* in the context established by the earlier novels reveals the excellence of Mr. Waugh's talent within his own comic tradition. The implication that this tradition is his natural métier follows from his obvious enjoyment of his task when he writes within it. The comic sections of this novel—the portraits of Ryder's father, Boy Mulcaster, Mr. Samgrass, the people Ryder meets aboard the ship, Bridey, the visit to the Old Hundredth, Sebastian triumphantly drunk among the dogmatic houyhnhnms of the Brideshead drawing room—all have a spontaneous lift and freshness which is lacking in other parts of the novel. The best of *Brideshead Revisited* belongs with the earlier tradition; left with the reader are passages of empty rhetoric and the feeling that an attempt to force a serious frame of reference upon an unconscious use of the comic tradition has not been entirely successful.

NOTES

1 Erwin Stürzl, "Evelyn Waugh's Romanwork: Makabre Farce oder 'Menschliche Komödie?' " *Die Neueren Sprachen,* VIII (July, 1959), 318.

2 Frederick J. Stopp, *Evelyn Waugh: Portrait of an Artist* (London: Chapman and Hall, 1958), p. 76.

3 Evelyn Waugh, *Brideshead Revisited* (Boston: Little, Brown & Co., 1946), p. 350. See also Stopp, pp. 205-206.

4 Evelyn Waugh, *Decline and Fall* (Boston: Little, Brown & Co., 1946), p. 162. Almost all of Chapter II of Part II is given to this statement.

5 Evelyn Waugh, *Vile Bodies* (Boston: Little, Brown & Co., 1946), p. 183.

6 Richard J. Voorhees, "Evelyn Waugh Revisited," *South Atlantic Quarterly,* XLVIII (April, 1949), 279-280.

7 Stephen Spender, *The Creative Element* (New York: British Book Center, 1954), p. 174.

8 A. E. Dyson, "Evelyn Waugh and the Mysteriously Disappearing Hero," *Critical Quarterly,* II (Spring, 1960), 77.

9 A. J. Neame, "Black and Blue: a Study of the Catholic Novel," *The European,* April, 1953, p. 36.

Bernard Bergonzi

EVELYN WAUGH'S GENTLEMAN

There is a view of Evelyn Waugh's fiction which is becoming increasingly familiar. It was outlined by Conor Cruise O'Brien in his book *Maria Cross* (first published under the pseudonym of 'Donat O'Donnell' in 1953); and was more recently stated by Frank Kermode in 'Mr. Waugh's Cities', *Puzzles and Epiphanies* (1962). This view sees Waugh as turning quite early from the nihilistic fun of his first two novels, *Decline and Fall* and *Vile Bodies,* to a kind of Tory romanticism, evident as early as 1934 in *A Handful of Dust.* Here, in the figure of Tony Last, we see the first outlines of the English Gothic dream, the cult of the aristocracy and the country house. In *Brideshead Revisited* (1945) this dream developed into a total myth; the aristocracy—particularly the Catholic aristocracy—were seen as the unique custodians of the traditional values in a world increasingly threatened by the barbarians, personified in the uncouth young officer, Hooper. In Frank Kermode's words, 'The great houses of England become by an easy transition types of the Catholic city'. The point is made explicit at several crucial moments in *Brideshead,* when we are reminded of the great lamentation sung during Holy Week, *Quomodo sedet sola civitas*—"How doth the city sit solitary that was full of people"—echoing the decline of Brideshead Castle and the values it enshrined. *Brideshead Revisited* first established Evelyn Waugh as a "Catholic novelist" (to use a term that is surely something of a kiss of death), but many readers

From *Critical Quarterly*, V (Spring 1963), 23-36. Reprinted by permission of the author.

found his association of Catholicism and aristocratic virtues, the identification of House and City, arbitrary in the extreme. O'Brien has, in fact, referred to "Mr. Waugh's private religion, on which he has superimposed Catholicism, much as newly converted pagans are said to superimpose a Christian nomenclature on their ancient cults of trees and thunder."

On the whole, one can accept this analysis. It is impossible to read *A Handful of Dust* and then *Brideshead Revisited* without feeling the force of Mr. Waugh's personal myth, in which the precise role of Catholicism, is to say the least of it, ambiguous (though to say this isn't, of course, to cast any doubt on the sincerity of Mr. Waugh's personal attachment to the Catholic religion). But I would also like to suggest that the myth is less simple than some critics have suggested, and that Waugh's own attitude to it isn't altogether straight-forward. More significant, however, are the implications of his latest novel, *Unconditional Surrender,* [1] published in 1961. This completes the Crouchback Trilogy, (now known as *Sword of Honour*) begun in 1952, of which the first two sections were *Men at Arms* and *Officers and Gentlemen.* The three works add up to an uneven but, I think, extremely impressive long novel of nearly a thousand pages, which diminishes, in several senses, *Brideshead Revisited,* and which must inevitably change our whole picture of Mr. Waugh's fictional development. And with the completion of the Crouchback trilogy, the romantic and aristocratic myth, previously so dominating, is totally transformed. I would like to re-examine what one may loosely call Mr. Waugh's "serious novels" in the new perspective that the Crouchback triology offers us.

To return, first, to *A Handful of Dust.* Frank Kermode has referred to it as "one of the most distinguished novels of the century"; this is high praise, but I am inclined to agree. Nevertheless, another critic, Graham Martin, writing in *The Modern Age,* the final volume of the *Pelican*

Guide to English Literature, has confessed himself puzzled by such valuations. He objects that the book is all surface, that when one tries to probe beneath it to discover the reality of the Lasts' marital tragedy one finds nothing: "We are manipulated into accepting as 'real' characterizations and substantial moral involvements people and a story that are scarcely there at all." Mr. Martin is complaining that *A Handful of Dust* can't be serious because it lacks the three-dimensional solidity of the conventionally serious novel. Yet looking at the book another way one might argue that its success partly stems from the fact that Waugh is able to do so much with so little. In its essential method it doesn't greatly differ from the early farces, *Decline and Fall* and *Vile Bodies*: the characters are puppets, caricatures, pasteboard figures, rather than fully-rounded characters. This is certainly true of John Beaver and Brenda Last; and is largely so of the hero, Tony Last. There is rather more to him, more, perhaps, to involve our sympathies, but he still remains a shadowy figure, the stylized embodiment of a number of predictable gestures. Nevertheless, the total effect of the book is certainly different from that of its two predecessors. The farce is very evident, and it is as cruel as ever—Mr. Waugh's comedy is characteristically cruel, and many readers are squeamish about it; but cruelty is of the essence of most farce, as Bergson long ago pointed out. But the farce strangely co-exists with something very different, an intense pathos that would be tragic if the characters involved had a sufficient degree of humanity to support tragedy. In presenting their inability to do so, Waugh is, I think, making a searching though wholly implicit moral comment on the empty world of the Lasts and the Beavers. The characters have something of the inability to feel deeply that marks the inhabitants of Eliot's *Waste Land,* as the use of a quotation from that poem to form the book's title may remind us. At the end of the novel farce deepens into horror, as we leave Tony Last imprisoned forever in the South American jungle reading Dickens to

71

the recluse, Mr. Todd. It is true that no one specific response is called up and sustained as we are reading *A Handful of Dust,* which is something that Mr. Martin complains of, but if one is to come to terms with Waugh one has to accept the fact that he frequently calls forth multiple responses which may often neutralize or contradict each other. It is, it seems to me, an acceptable attitude to the complexity and ambiguity of experience, a justifiable refusal to narrow down one's response to a single, sharply-defined moral attitude. *A Handful of Dust* is a farce in Bergsonian terms: we laugh at people, or objects resembling people, colliding like things. But we are disconcerted by realising almost simultaneously that these seemingly mechanical semblances of humanity *are* really persons, or very nearly so. Tony Last embodies the pathos of the wooden puppet that suddenly weeps real tears.

The mixture of farce and seriousness in *A Handful of Dust* gives the book its peculiar strength. It is a combination which recurs in the Crouchback trilogy, but is almost entirely lacking in *Brideshead Revisited,* to the detriment of that work. Certainly, *A Handful of Dust* is much less of a *novel* than either of these; it is rather a mixture of farce and myth or romance. And Tony Last, if he lacks the depth and complexity of a major fictional character, does have the broad, simple outlines of a hero of myth. As his perhaps too obviously symbolic name implies, he is the ultimate survivor of a former age and scheme of values, whom nobody understands, least of all his wife, Brenda. He is too good for the world he is born into, and a predestined victim, a scapegoat cast out to a living death in the wilderness. Like most of Waugh's heroes—with the notable exception of Basil Seal—he is also slightly stupid. If he is the last wistful inheritor of a noble tradition, he is also singularly lacking in a sense of reality; and as Kermode has noted, Waugh is hard on such characters. This ambivalence is something that recurs in Waugh's fiction, and which prevents him from accepting quite unreservedly the aristocratic myth.

Certainly Hetton Abbey, the country seat to which Tony Last is so attached, is less intrinsically impressive than Brideshead or Broome. In the words of the local guide-book, "This, formerly one of the notable houses of the county, was entirely rebuilt in 1864 in the Gothic style, and is now devoid of interest." Nevertheless Tony preserves a passionate devotion to it:

But there was not a glazed brick or encaustic tile that was not dear to Tony's heart. In some ways, he knew, it was not convenient to run; but what big house was? It was not altogether amenable to modern ideas of comfort; he had many small improvements in mind, which would be put into effect as soon as the death duties were paid off. But the general aspect and atmosphere of the place; the line of its battlements against the sky; the central clock tower where quarterly chimes disturbed all but the heaviest of sleepers; the ecclesiastical gloom of the great hall, its ceiling groined and painted in diapers of red and gold, supported on shafts of polished granite with vine-wreathed capitals, half-lit by day through lancet windows of armorial stained glass, at night by a vast gasolier of brass and wrought iron, wired now and fitted with twenty electric bulbs; the blasts of hot air that rose suddenly at one's feet, through grills of cast-iron trefoils from the antiquated heating apparatus below; the cavernous chill of the more remote corridors where, economizing in coke, he had had the pipes shut off; the dining-hall with its hammer-beam roof and pitch-pine minstrels' gallery; the bedrooms with their brass bedsteads, each with a frieze of Gothic text, each named from Malory, Yseult, Elaine, Mordred and Merlin, Gawaine and Bedivere, Lancelot, Perceval, Tristram, Galahad, his own dressing-room, Morgan le Fay, and Brenda's Guinevere, where the bed stood on a dais, the walls were hung with tapestry, the fireplace was like a tomb of the thirteenth century, from whose bay windows one could count, on days of exceptional clearness, the spires of six churches—all these things with which he had grown up were a source of constant delight and exultation to Tony; things of tender memory and proud possession.

In this description of the Victorian Gothic splendors of Hetton, we are aware of the intensity of Tony's affections, but we also see that the objects to which they are directed are slightly preposterous. His bogus Pre-Raphaelite world cuts him off from the wider past, just as his conventional Anglicanism cuts him off from genuine religion; when Tony's son has been killed in a hunting accident the local vicar attempts to solace him, but Tony complains, "I only tried to see him about arrangements. He tried to be comforting. It was very painful . . . after all the last thing one wants to talk about at a time like this is religion."

Tony Last offers only a dim foreshadowing of Guy Crouchback, who is Waugh's fully developed picture of the Christian gentleman, the doomed victim of the modern world. But there are still a number of direct anticipations. One of them is in the romantic harking-back to the attitudes of the nursery and the schoolroom which, as O'Brien has remarked, runs through several of Waugh's novels: one thinks of Sebastian Flyte's teddy-bear, and the way in which Brideshead Castle is quietly presided over by the old nurse Nanny Hawkins, like a tutelary deity in a remote upper room. Last preserves quite unashamedly in his bedroom various treasures of boyhood: "the framed picture of a dreadnought (a colored supplement from *Chums*), all its guns spouting flame and smoke; a photographic group of his private school; a cabinet call "the Museum," filled with the fruits of a dozen desultory hobbies, eggs, butterflies, fossils, coins." In *Men at Arms,* Guy Crouchback, before his various disillusionments, is reminded when he hears the phrase, "tomorrow you meet the men you will lead in battle," of a hero of boyhood adventure stories called Captain Truslove, whose exploits had fascinated him at his preparatory school during the First World War.

Again, in *A Handful of Dust,* Tony Last hears from Dr. Messinger of a fabulous city in the Brazilian hinterland, and he agrees to join Messinger's expedition in search of it. Tony soon translates this City into familiar terms:

He had a clear picture of it in his mind. It was Gothic in character, all vanes and pinnacles, gargoyles, battlements, groin-

74

ing and tracery, pavilions and terraces, a transfigured Hetton, pennons and banners floating on the sweet breeze, everything luminous and translucent; a coral citadel crowning a green hill-top sown with heraldic and fabulous animals and symmetrical, disproportionate blossom.

This is an aesthetic fantasy rather than the Catholic City of *Brideshead* or *Helena;* but it is indeed 'a transfigured Hetton', and seems medieval and therefore Catholic— reminiscent perhaps of the Green Knight's castle when Sir Gawaine first encounters it—unlike the bogus Victorian Gothic of the actual Hetton.

Catholicism as such does not enter Waugh's fiction until *Brideshead,* but in 1935 he published his terse, distinguished life of Edmund Campion, which made apparent his own religious commitments, and showed that he was capable of a kind of writing very different indeed from the farcical novels which had established his reputation. From the point of view of Waugh's later work, *Edmund Campion* is interesting because it shows, for the first time, his feeling for the recusant families who, despite immeasurable difficulties, had kept the Catholic faith alive in England for three centuries; we are later to see them celebrated in Lady Marchmain's family, and in the Crouchbacks, one of those forebears, Blessed Gervase Crouchback, had, like Campion, been martyred under Elizabeth.

The Campion biography, combined with the hints of gravity in *A Handful of Dust,* might have suggested that Waugh would one day attempt a novel of high seriousness. Nevertheless, when such a novel was finally written, in the form of *Brideshead Revisited,* many readers were disconcerted. Mr. Waugh has remarked that it "lost me such esteem as I once enjoyed among my contemporaries." This long, lush, glittering story about an aristocratic Catholic family between the wars, seen through the eyes of an all too obviously fascinated hanger-on, who is the intimate friend of one of them and becomes the lover of another, was rather too much for many readers, even those who had most enjoyed the comic novels. And Catholicism pervaded the whole work, culminating in the death-bed repentance of the long-estranged Lord Marchmain. In his preface to the recently revised edition of this novel, Mr. Waugh remarks that though he makes no apology for the theme of the book, "the operation of divine grace on a group of diverse but closely connected characters," he is not altogether happy with its form, but sees no way of radically transforming it. The cuts and revisions that he has made in the new edition are interesting but not extensive. Mr. Waugh explains that his book was written in the early months of 1944:

It was a bleak period of present privation and threatening disaster—the period of soya beans and basic English— and in consequence the book is infused with a kind of gluttony, for food and wine, for the splendours of the recent past, and for rhetorical and ornamental language, which now with a full stomach I find distasteful. I have modified the grosser passages but have not obliterated them because they are an essential part of the book.

Thus we find that the glamorous impression that Anthony Blanche makes on Charles Ryder in Oxford is somewhat toned down; while the prose poem in praise of Burgundy that occurs during Ryder's dinner with Rex Mottram—a decidedly overwritten piece—has been sensibly reduced.

One of the most interesting changes concerns the crucial paragraph in which Julia, on an ocean liner, first becomes Charles's mistress. In its original version the passage read as follows:

So at sunset I took formal possession of her as her lover. It was no time for the sweets of luxury; they would come, in their season, with the swallow and the lime flowers. Now on the rough water, as I was made free of her narrow loins and, it seemed now, in assuaging that fierce appetite, cast a burden which I had borne all my life, toiled under, not knowing its nature—now, while the waves still broke and thundered on

76

the prow, the act of possession was a symbol, a rite of ancient origin and solemn meaning.

This is a fairly lush passage, but no more so than many others. Yet it shows that for Charles becoming Julia's lover was not just a personal transaction, but had a ritualistic, even a religious significance—"the act of possession was a symbol, a rite of ancient origin and solemn meaning." He is not merely taking possession of Julia as a woman, but is becoming carnally incorporated into the magic circle of Brideshead, a kind of earthly beatitude. It's not surprising that Mr. Waugh realised the exceedingly vulnerable implications of all this, though I'm not sure that the new version offers a fundamental improvement:

It was no time for the sweets of luxury: they would come in their season with the swallow and the lime flowers. Now on the rough water there was a formality to be observed, no more. It was as though a deed of conveyance of her narrow loins had been drawn and sealed. I was making my first entry as the freeholder of a property I would enjoy and develop at leisure.

The tone is now, it will be seen, more restrained; and instead of a "rite of ancient origin" we have the taking legal possession of a property. Yet in its larger context the implications of this relatively more mundane imagery are curious and surely unfortunate. For there is a point, a little later in the novel, when it seems that Charles, from having taken possession of Julia, is about to take possession of Brideshead Castle itself: Charles and Julia are being divorced from their respective partners and intend to marry as soon as they can; while dying Lord Marchmain, disgusted by his son Brideshead's unfortunate marriage, is bequeathing the property to Julia. In the event, things work out otherwise; when her father dies Julia returns to the practice of her religion and doesn't marry Charles. Nevertheless, Mr. Waugh's revision of this paragraph still suggests that for Charles Julia could never be just a woman he was in love with. She inevitably stood for much more—for Brideshead Castle and all its treasure, both material and spiritual. Such revisions as Mr. Waugh has made, once one examines them, have the possibly unwelcome effect of drawing attention to the weak points in the narrative, showing where the author felt a certain need to tamper with the story. It is, on the whole, questionable whether the novel has gained very much from these changes. Yet Mr. Waugh's preface does revealingly suggest that we are to read *Brideshead Revisited* "as a souvenir of the Second War rather than one of the twenties or of the thirties, with which it ostensibly deals." This, and the previous observation about the work being a product of the "present privation and the threatening disaster of wartime," though made with disarming modesty, must inevitably alter our view of *Brideshead*.

It becomes, in short, much less of a sober chronicle of grace and adultery and aristocratic folly between the wars, and much more an almost uncontrolled fantasy. Here, as in other matters, Waugh's latest work, *Unconditional Surrender,* affords appropriate illumination. Consider the account of Major Ludovic's fabulous novel, *The Death Wish,* written at much the same time as *Brideshead*:

It was a very gorgeous, almost gaudy, tale of romance and high drama. . . . Had he known it, half a dozen other English writers, averting themselves sickly from privations of war and apprehensions of the social consequences of peace, were even then severally and secretly, unknown to one another, composing or preparing to compose books which would turn from the drab alleys of the thirties into the odorous gardens of a recent past transformed and illuminated by disordered memory and imagination.

Is it unfair to conclude that Major Ludovic and Mr. Waugh were both writing the same kind of book? The conclusion seems to me inescapable. Significant, too, is the phrase "transformed and illuminated by disordered memory and imagination." *Brideshead Revisited,* one remembers, is subtitled, "The Sacred and Profane Memories of Captain Charles Ryder." The whole Marchmain saga is related through memories, certainly drenched with nostalgia and quite possibly disordered, of Charles Ryder. And Ryder is, unfortunately, one of Mr. Waugh's least interesting characters: weak, sentimental, snobbish. Even such a devoted admirer of Waugh's work as Mr. F. J. Stopp refers in his book on Waugh to "a streak of maudlin sentimentality about Charles." Certainly the story suffers through being filtered through the sadly limited consciousness of Ryder; the events can scarcely transcend the personality of their narrator (what, I sometimes thought, if Ryder were a liar as well as a sentimentalist; supposing he had made it all up, as part of a huge wish-fulfillment fantasy, had scarcely even known the Marchmains, perhaps merely admired Sebastian at a distance at Oxford?). And for much of the time, one must admit, Waugh is identified altogether too closely with his narrator. But not entirely so; part of the conscience of the book is embodied in the engaging but astringent personality of Anthony Blanche, who gives Charles solemn warnings against falling a victim to the fatal charm of the Marchmains, warnings which Charles inevitably disregards. Mr. Stopp refers to a possible division in Waugh's own attitude:

Perhaps, even, Sebastian and Anthony represent the two contrasted sides of Mr. Waugh's own writing—always balanced and at loggerheads, usually holding each other in strict check, the one tempting to indiscretion, the other leering at the lush scene through an *oeuil de boeuf,* the one erring disconsolately, banished from his arcadian home, the other wandering insatiably, an inhabitant of all climes and of none.

One could, I think, have done with rather more of Anthony Blanche and his detached vision.

As O'Brien has pointed out, Waugh was attempting, in *Brideshead,* an elaborate Proustian recreation of time past for which his talents were fundamentally ill-suited. Much of the book's elaborate metaphorical structure seems to me merely superimposed rather than integral. Above all, the absence of Mr. Waugh's comic genius is a grave weakness. Nevertheless, when all this is admitted, enough remains to make the novel a far from insignificant work. It is admirably planned and constructed, the characters, though often distorted by Ryder's view of them, are convincing—and in Julia, Waugh has invented an attractive female character of, for him, unusual depth and complexity. And in the early Oxford chapters the magic that Charles found there, and the glamour of the young Sebastian, is, for me at least, effectively conveyed. (Though for an index of the way in which time and circumstance have blurred and softened Mr. Waugh's vision one need only compare the Oxford of *Brideshead* with the Oxford of the opening chapter of *Decline and Fall*). And, like other Catholic readers, I find the working out of the theme of grace, culminating in the death-bed reconciliation of Lord Marchmain and Julia's sacrifice of Charles, credible and indeed moving; though one must also recognise that many other readers find this objectionably contrived; here, however, one is entering on territory that lies far beyond literary discussion.

In *Brideshead Revisited* the tendency to myth-making, first evident in *A Handful of Dust,* becomes total and all-embracing. And reading *Brideshead* we have to think of the word "myth" not only in its larger positive sense but also, such are the insufficiencies of Ryder, in the everyday pejorative sense of "illusion." At one point Ryder confesses his inability to live in a world without illusions:

'I have left behind illusion,' I said to myself. 'Henceforth I live in the world of three dimensions—with the aid of my five senses.'
I have since learned that there is no such world, but then, as the car turned out of sight of the house, I thought it took no finding, but lay all about me at the end of the avenue.

Nevertheless, the fact that a world of three-dimensional

reality, seen without myth or illusion, *is* possible, is shown by Mr. Waugh's next serious novel, *Helena* (1950). This is an odd and in many respects unsatisfactory book, but I'm not concerned, at the moment, with making a detailed assessment of its literary merits. Thematically it is of marked interest, since it shows a totally different aspect of Mr. Waugh's universe from *Brideshead;* if that work had been oriented toward myth, *Helena* shows us his concern for naked unadorned reality. The Empress Helena searching in old age for the True Cross, is above all concerned with establishing the historical reality of Christianity. Christ lived and died in a particular place, at a particular time, and the cross on which he died was simply two pieces of ordinary wood. Helena insists on the ordinariness of the cross during her search, in the face of the pious sages who claim that it was made of every species of wood so that all the vegetable world could participate in the act of redemption; or that it was composed equally of cypress, cedar, boxwood and pine, with appropriate symbolic associations; or that it was made of aspen, which is why that tree now continually shivers with shame. To all these ingenious speculations Helena, with anti-mythical zest, replies "Nonsense" or "Rot." Similarly, she resists the attempts of her son, Constantine, to mythologize the truths of Christianity. Again, we can compare the extreme selectivity of the Catholic City in *Brideshead* with Helena's desire to extend the City far beyond the Roman Empire to all mankind. In *Helena* Mr. Waugh is writing of matters that are very remote from his customary fictional interests, and perhaps for that reason he is able to assert an anti-mythical attitude with remarkable clarity. It is a new note in his work, and in the Crouchback trilogy we see the struggle between myth and "three-dimensional reality" through to its conclusion.

It is instructive to approach *Men at Arms,* the first volume of the trilogy, via *Put Out More Flags* (1942) which also deals with the Phony War of 1939-40, though written much closer to the period it describes. It is one of

Waugh's funniest novels, in which we finally take leave of the denizens of his early fiction, Sir Alastair Digby-Vaine-Trumpington and Basil Seal. For a time no one takes the war seriously; Basil, who wants to be one of the hard-faced men who did well out of the war, stays in the country indulging in various profitable rackets, while Alastair enjoys the glorious lark of joining up as a ranker because he can't bear to meet the temporary officers—though presumably the era of Hooper was still some way ahead. After the fall of France, however, things liven up, and both Basil and Alastair take commissions in a branch of the army that is being formed for special service. Alastair describes it in these words:

'They're getting up special parties for raiding. They go across to France and creep up behind Germans and cut their throats in the dark.' He was very excited, turning a page in his life, as, more than twenty years ago lying on his stomach before the fire, with a bound volume of *Chums,* he used to turn over to the next instalment of the serial.

We are in familiar territory, the world of the schoolboy heroics; it looks back to Tony Last, whose framed picture of a dreadnought had been taken from a color supplement of the same magazine, *Chums;* and forward to Guy Crouchback, remembering the intrepid Captain Truslove. As the novel closes we leave Basil and Alastair about to embark on wonderful romantic adventures; the Phony War is over and England is inspirited by the Churchillian Renaissance. Sir Joseph Mainwaring, who has been wrong about everything so far, remarks, "There's a new spirit abroad. I see it on every side." And the author comments, in the last line of the novel, 'And, poor booby, he was bang right.'

In *Men at Arms* and *Officers and Gentlemen* the Commando group that Alastair refers to so enthusiastically is described in much greater detail. It is known as HOO—Hazardous Offensive Operations—and though it provides plenty of grim comedy, it offers very little of the simple schoolboy heroics of Alastair's eager description.

Indeed, one of the most remarkable things about the Crouchback trilogy is that though the work of an author of extreme right-wing opinions it is one of the most thorough-going satires of military life on record. Guy Crouchback's military career is totally inglorious if for no fault of his own. The military operations recorded are either failures, like the raid on Dakar or the evacuation from Crete; or else they are put-up jobs, designed solely for propaganda purposes, like Trimmer's ludicrous raid on the coast of Occupied France, or the attack on the Croatian block-house in *Unconditional Surrender*. The first and third volumes are dominated by two figures who, though wonderful as fictional characters, offer between them as gross a caricature of the ideal of the officer and gentleman as one could imagine—Apthorpe and Ludovic. Those who do not seem to embody this ideal betray it, voluntarily or involuntarily. By the end of the novel what had started as a clear-cut fight against Evil has become hopelessly enmeshed in politics and rival fanaticisms.

At the opening of *Men at Arms* we are introduced to Guy Crouchback, the mild, melancholy Catholic gentleman who has lived in Italy ever since his wife left him several years before. He has elements of Tony Last about him, as well as of Charles Ryder and the Marchmain ethos. With the Russo-German pact in 1939 Guy finds many issues crystallized, and he returns to England eager for a place in the fight:

But now, splendidly, everything had become clear. The enemy at last was plain in view, huge and hateful, all disguise cast off. It was the Modern Age in arms. Whatever the outcome there was a place for him in that battle.

Before leaving Italy he takes a significant step back into the past, like Ortega y Gasset's ancient Roman. He kneels in the local church and prays at the effigy of an English knight, Sir Roger of Waybroke, who had been shipwrecked on the way to the Second Crusade: " 'Sir Roger, pray for me,' he said, 'and for our endangered kingdom'."

Charles Ryder too, we remember, had looked back into the past though in a rather more pretentious way; he had complained that "Hooper was no romantic. He had not as a child ridden with Rupert's horse or sat among the camp fires at Xanthus-side." As we have seen, Crouchback in his early days as an officer thinks about and even identifies himself with the gallant Captain Truslove of his boyhood reading. But unlike Ryder he changes and learns. There can be no doubt of Mr. Waugh's intense sympathy for Crouchback; but Crouchback is also judged; and he learns to judge himself. The process culminates most impressively in *Unconditional Surrender*. But even in the earlier volumes there are signs of it. In *Men at Arms* Guy is constrained to ask the pious Catholic genealogist, Mr. Goodall, "do you seriously believe that God's Providence concerns itself with the perpetuation of the English Catholic aristocracy?" Mr. Goodall returns with a neat answer, "But, of course. And with sparrows too, we are taught." Nevertheless, the fact that the question could be formulated and asked at all, and by Guy, shows that Waugh is writing with a degree of detachment that is lacking in *Brideshead*. The hard outlines of reality are everywhere visible in the Crouchback books. In the person of Mr. Goodall Waugh amusingly satirises the romantic political fantasies of certain Catholics:

Guy visited Mr. Goodall and found him elated by the belief that a great rising was imminent throughout Christian Europe; led by the priests and squires, with blessed banners, and the relics of the saints borne ahead, Poles, Hungarians, Austrians, Bavarians, Italians and plucky little contingents from the Catholic cantons of Switzerland would soon be on the march to redeem the times. Even a few Frenchmen, Mr. Goodall conceded, might join this Pilgrimage of Grace but he could promise no part in it for Guy.

Despite his romanticism, Guy realizes the absurdity of such dreams; that he does so places him squarely on the side of "three-dimensional reality" against the myth-makers, with large implications for the latter part of the story.

In *Unconditional Surrender* Guy's Uncle Peregrine plays a similar part to Mr. Goodall; reading the war news he complains that the Bolshevists are advancing and that the Germans seem unable to stop them: "I'd sooner see the Japanese in Europe—at least they have a king and some sort of religion." Though here Waugh's irony is characteristically double-edged; we smile at the political naivete, but perhaps also wonder uneasily whether the Japanese in Europe *would* have been particularly worse than the Russians.

In the person of Guy Crouchback Waugh offers us his fullest and most sympathetic delineation of the ideal of the Gentleman, the embodiment of the Gothic dream, a gallant officer who would be, if he could, a twentieth-century reincarnation of Roger of Waybroke. The trilogy shows us first his disillusionment and then the total defeat of his ideal by the inescapable forces of modern war. And Waugh traces the various stages in his disillusionment with subtlety and most ingenious irony; there are many traps for the unwary reader. During the Cretan campaign Corporal-Major Ludovic notes in his diary: "Captain Crouchback is pleased because General Miltiades is a gentleman. He would like to believe that the war is being fought by such. But all gentlemen are now very old." Later Ludovic, as the author of *The Death Wish,* is to become an arch mythmaker; but here he is doing no more than wryly record what Guy has to recognize as the sober truth.

Guy has already heard the same thing, in more hectoring terms, from Ian Killbannock, the journalist-peer turned Government propaganist:

'You'll see pages about the Commandos in the papers soon. But not about your racket, Guy. They just won't do, you know. Delightful fellows, heroes too, I daresay, but the Wrong Period. Last-war stuff, Guy. Went out with Rupert Brooke.'

'You find us poetic?'

'No,' said Ian, stopping in his path and turning to face Guy in the darkness. 'Perhaps not poetic, exactly, but Upper Class.

Hopelessly Upper Class. You're the "Fine Flower of the Nation". You can't deny it and *it won't do.*'

The immediate response to this, by a reader familiar with Waugh's other fiction and in sympathy with his ideals, would be to assume that Killbannock is being a boor, that the ideals he is attacking are nevertheless admirable, and that the phrase "Fine Flower of the Nation" remains valid despite his sarcastic contempt. We think of the gay adventurers of the end of *Put Out More Flags,* and of the solemn visions of Charles Ryder, remembering perhaps his account of the three brothers of Lady Marchmain, killed in the First World War: "garlanded victims, devoted to sacrifice. These men must die to make a world for Hooper." And a little later we find Crouchback doing precisely this, thinking about Ivor Claire, in language that would have wholly appropriate to Charles Ryder:

Guy remembered Claire as he first saw him in the Roman spring in the afternoon sunlight amid the embosoming cypresses of the Borghese Gardens, putting his horse faultlessly over the jumps, concentrated as a man in prayer. Ivor Claire, Guy thought, was the fine flower of them all. He was quintessential England, the man Hitler had not taken into account.

And how wrong Guy is. In the Cretan campaign Ivor Claire deserts in the face of the enemy. The profundity of Guy's wrongness has immensely far-reaching implications. If the quintessential gentleman is not to be trusted then the whole scheme of values that has so far pervaded Waugh's serious fiction falls to the ground. An Ivor Claire is not necessarily better than a Hooper or a Trimmer, and the hero-worshipping of a Charles Ryder becomes altogether suspect.

Guy's disillusion is completed in *Unconditional Surrender.* His mission to the Yugoslav partisans is as much concerned with establishing political tyranny as with defeating the forces of evil. The splendid vision with which he started the war in *Men at Arms* is wholly obscured.

"This isn't soldiering as I was taught it," remarks a British officer when forced to acquiesce in the liquidation of a Yugoslav royalist. Guy is heavily involved in the prevalent betrayals, even if inadvertently. In Yugoslavia he learns, finally, the meaning of total war. Towards the end of the book he is addressed by a Hungarian woman, a Jewish refugee, in these terms:

'Is there any place that is free from evil? It is too simple to say that only the Nazis wanted war. These communists wanted it too. It was the only way in which they could come to power. Many of my people wanted it, to be revenged on the Germans, to hasten the creation of the national state. It seems to me there was a will to war, a death wish, everywhere. They could assert their manhood by killing and being killed. They would accept hardships in recompense for being selfish and lazy. Danger justified privilege. I knew Italians—not very many perhaps —who felt this. Were there none in England?

'God forgive me,' said Guy. 'I was one of them.'

At this point Guy's self-knowledge is complete, and the dominating myth of much of Waugh's work is deflated. Reality is too terrible and too various to be accounted for by any simple myth, any easy patterns of heroics, no matter how splendid. Already we have seen Guy's devout and humble father exhibiting the realistic Christianity of a Helena rather than the mythologized version of the March-mains. The romantic ideal of the gentleman, of the fine flower of the nation, may indeed have undergone an unconditional surrender. But there are other, more elementary and perhaps sounder values. At the end of the novel we find Guy married to the earthy and tractor-driving Domenica Plessington, who has borne him two sons. But the heir to Broome and to the venerable name of Crouchback is little Trimmer, son of the man who was in all respects the total antithesis of the gentlemanly ideal. This is, on the face of it, one of Mr. Waugh's most savagely sardonic ironies of situation. Yet, as old Mr. Crouchback would surely have observed, even a Trimmer has a soul to be saved, and his child is being brought up in the Faith; has become an inhabitant of the City in Helena's sense rather than the Marchmains'. Is it fanciful to conclude that Guy's heir represents a union, no matter how oddly contrived, between the Upper Classes and the People, and that he embodies, too, Mr. Waugh's final, infinitely reluctant surrender to the modern world?

Postscript 1968: Some of the passages quoted from the separate volumes of *Sword of Honour* no longer appear in the revised one-volume edition published in 1965.

NOTE

1 The American edition is called *The End of the Battle*.

Robert Murray Davis

THE MIND AND ART OF EVELYN WAUGH

With the death of Evelyn Waugh on Easter Sunday of 1966, the body of his work has been given not only a beginning and a middle but a definite end. As a result, critics of his novels must find a new perspective. No longer can they point to his brilliant promise or qualify judicious praise of his later work with hopes that his talent will yet revive and flower and that his next book, by abandoning pretensions to serious treatment of moral, religious, and social themes, will repeat the artistic triumph of books written twenty years earlier. Now the process of selection must begin: work of enduring value must be separated from the dross inevitable in the work of any busy artist. It is too early, of course, to attempt a final estimate of Waugh's novels. However, they are clearly worth estimating and then subjecting to further study, and it is not too early to indicate some of the grounds upon which judgments can be made and to point to some necessary critical and scholarly tasks.

I

Despite the amount of critical attention that Waugh has received, a number of obvious but important matters still deserve attention. [1] Surprisingly enough, the art of individual novels has not been explored very thoroughly, nor have Waugh's method and style been examined in sufficient detail. Structure has received more attention than

From *Papers on Literature and Language,* III (Summer 1967), 270-287. Reprinted by permission of the publisher.

style, but a number of questions remain unanswered. For example, some ordinarily perceptive readers do not find a principle of unity in *A Handful of Dust,* which seems to them to alter radically in tone and method after the death of John Andrew Last. A similar question about unity or its lack could be raised about the introduction of Dame Mildred Porch in *Black Mischief.* Perhaps these objections can be answered on the grounds that not all novels should be expected to conform to Jamesian ideas of structure. At any rate, questions of unity cannot be ignored.

Waugh's intellectual and artistic opinions, particularly as exhibited in his nonfiction, have been outlined by a number of critics; further discussion should deal not only with his statements but with their historical, social, and intellectual context. For example, Waugh several times mentions Von Hügel; his works and those of other devotional writers might throw some light on Waugh's attitudes and even upon the structure of his novels, particularly the later ones. At least as important to a serious consideration of the novels are Waugh's views about society and its historical development. He frequently wrote of change and decay in modern civilization, and it could be argued that he was influenced by cyclic theories of history, notably those of Oswald Spengler. He owned a copy of *The Decline of the West* early in his career, and he would not have had to read very far to discover a passage which seems to presage *A Handful of Dust*:

In place of a world, there is a city, a point, in which the whole life of broad regions is collecting while the rest dries up. In place of a true-type people, born of and grown on the soil, there is a new sort of nomad, cohering unstably in fluid masses, the parasitical city dweller, traditionless, utterly matter-of-fact, religionless, clever, unfruitful, deeply contemptuous of the countryman and especially that highest form of countryman, the country gentleman. This is a very great stride towards the inorganic, towards the end.

This does not mean that Waugh was a follower of Spengler—it seems probable that he accepted Spengler's picture of modern society without assenting to Spengler's conclusions about the nature of man—but the kind and extent of the influence of this and other historical and political thinkers needs to be explored.

These problems can not, perhaps, be dealt with in satisfactory fashion until more is known about Waugh's life, and it is probably too early to expect a searching biography, though Christopher Sykes, if he carries out tentative plans to write the life, should produce a useful and interesting book. There are no serious obstacles to the compilation of a really thorough bibliography. Waugh certainly poses enough interesting problems to the bibliographer: his novels and even some of his travel books were published in a number of editions and states, and these and a number of fugitive items need to be gathered into a check-list. The textual scholar will have plenty to do, as the publishing history of *Brideshead Revisited* indicates. The novel first appeared in print in a special limited edition, and it may have been from this text that the serial version in *Town and Country* was derived. The texts of the English and American first editions—the primacy needs to be established—vary substantively in twenty-four places, and the 1960 revised edition, published only in England, contains more than 150 substantive variations from the first editions. The textual history of the other novels does not seem to be as complex, though it is sometimes nearly as long. Those histories should be established. [2] Doyle and Linck have already gathered some valuable information; both the English and American publishers have expressed willingness to provide information to bibliographers.

Except in this task, involving practical matters of physical evidence and requiring more industry than evaluation, scholars should proceed cautiously to examine the work carefully, to sift from the mass of inevitably repetitious criticism the genuine insights that it contains, and to expand their focus to place Waugh in the perspectives of the intellectual and literary history of the twentieth century and of the achievement of the great writers in the comic and satiric tradition. The critics—not necessarily a different group—should use this information and their own perceptions to give sympathetic and careful consideration of Waugh's strength as an artist as well as his limitations.

II

There is ample evidence that Waugh was aware of these limitations, for sporadically throughout his career he adopted a half-deprecating, half-defensive irony towards his work. In his first travel book, *A Bachelor Abroad,* he dwells on the mechanics of publicizing oneself as an author and laments the difficulty of finding "any aspect of social organization about which one can get down one's seventy thousand words without obvious plagiarism" (14). By 1934, he had reduced the travel book to a formula, and one can see from his comments in *Ninety-Two Days* and from his parody of that book in *Scoop* as John Boot's *Waste of Time* that the routine had become irksome to him. By the late 1930's, Waugh had become uncomfortably aware that his creative work had also been reduced to a conventional pattern. After the war came conflicting pronouncements on the writer as a sort of superior bootmaker, elegantly stitching together material in order to exchange the product for money and, conversely, on the writer as artist and seer, creating, unlike the politician, "a few objects of permanent value that were not there before him and would not have been there but for him" (*Tourist in Africa,* 187). The first mood tended to dominate when Waugh had finished a creative task, the second in periods of relative sterility. Near the end of his career, summing up the value of his education, he asserted that it had prepared him to become a writer of English prose —not a novelist or an artist, but a writer. It is tempting to apply to him his own analysis of Lactantius in *Helena,* that he "delighted in writing, in the joinery and embellishment of his sentences, in the consciousness of high rare virtue when every word had been used in its purest and most precise sense, in the kitten games of syntax and rhetoric. Words could do anything except generate their own meaning" (120).

Except generate their own meaning. This must come from the working of the artist's mind and imagination, not merely the craftsman's joinery, upon the world that he experiences. It has been argued that Waugh did not have the mind of a complete artist, and that his weaknesses as a novelist are the result. Certainly the cast of his mind, as exhibited in his writings, was exclusive rather than inclusive, more inclined to judgment than to sympathy, and more likely to illuminate strikingly a series of details than to shape and order those details into an artistically balanced whole. These characteristics — weaknesses in the view of many critics — can be traced readily enough, and one can agree thus far with his detractors: it is on the quality of his vision as shaped by his mind, not simply on his style, that Waugh's novels are going to stand or fall.

One of the traits of Waugh's character that was obvious to him as well as to his readers was his inability to sympathize with or even to understand those who did not share his tastes or his social class. Acknowledging a desire to be a man of the world in *They Were Still Dancing,* he admitted that he was scarcely fitted for the role in that "I shall always be ill at ease with nine out of every ten people I meet, that I shall always find something startling and rather abhorrent in the things most other people think worth doing and something puzzling in their standards of importance, that I shall probably be increasingly rather than decreasingly vulnerable to the inevitable minor disasters and injustices of life . . ." (143)—that, in sum, twenty-five years later he would become Gilbert Pinfold. This limitation of outlook seems to have been ingrained rather than assumed as an aspect of his persona. It is exemplified directly in his remark about the South American Indians who "moved invisibly like the tides, in some unexplained, pointless errand" or the Africans in mission schools, "with their rows of woolly black heads patiently absorbing 'education' " (*Ninety-Two Days*, 117, 111). Here Waugh lumps Indians and Africans into a mass and labels and dismisses them as being of little interest and no relevance to him. Even when he was moved to sympathy and interest—for English settlers in the highlands of Kenya, for Mexican landowners and peasants deprived of property and religion, and for the Masai and Arab cultures of East Africa—he seemed to be moved primarily by preconceived principles of class and racial solidarity, financial and religious sympathies, or an interest in coherent, picturesque social survivals that could pose no threat to his institutions and ideals, and he spent at least as much energy to denounce their opponents as to support their cause.

Whether cause, effect, or condition, Waugh's inability to identify with other people or groups was accompanied by his tendency to classify, analyze, separate, and judge. The clearest evidence of these habits of mind is provided by his biographies, where aspects of the subject's life are sorted into discrete compartments and presented as a series of activities rather than as a complex whole, contradictory and confusing, but vital. This tendency is as marked in his first book, the life of Rossetti, as in his last, *A Little Learning*. Presenting a phase of Rossetti's life, Waugh composed a series of essays, first on his relations with Ruskin, then with Morris and Burne-Jones, then with Elizabeth Siddal—and then, as if it were a wholly separate matter, he discussed Rossetti's career as a painter (67-91). There is little doubt that to some extent one's life is lived in compartments and that at any rate such a process is useful in bringing order to the biographer's material, but Waugh seems to have felt that such divisions spoke the whole truth about the way life is lived. *A Little Learning* contains the most striking illustration: "Under 'environment' I have included all the memories of childhood and some of my boyhood as it was lived at home.

School . . . was for the following eight years a different world, sometimes agreeable, more often not, inhabited by a quite different and rather nastier little boy who had no share in the real life of the third of a year he spent at home" (62). It is not strange that as a young man Waugh should hold this view; for a man nearing sixty, it is more remarkable.

The tendency to divide and classify operated in much of his writing. He declared in an essay in *Noblesse Oblige* that "Impotence and sodomy are socially OK, but birth control is flagrantly middle class" (71). In *Decline and Fall*, Otto Silenus divided people into the classes static and dynamic; in *A Handful of Dust,* Waugh divided mankind into the classes Tony Last and the others; and Charles Ryder saw an impassable gulf between Hooper, the representative of modern youth, and the brothers of Lady Marchmain in *Brideshead Revisited.* Even in the *Sword of Honour* trilogy, Waugh showed that old Mr. Crouchback and his landlords belong almost to different species. After their shoddy machinations fail and Mr. Crouchback's innocent magnanimity is revealed, the proprietor of the hotel tells his wife, "I never have understood him, not properly. Somehow his mind seems to work different than yours and mine" (301).

As a mental operation, classification involves both abstraction and distinction; distinction necessitates qualification—the addition of characteristics to differentiate one type from another—and the more complex but related operation, discrimination, involves judgment. From these basic habits of mind stem Waugh's choice of subject, his attitude toward it, and at least some features of the style and technique in which he embodied it. Leaving aside for the moment larger questions of subject matter, one can see clearly enough the effect of his way of thinking upon his means of creating characters. In the first edition of *Work Suspended,* he spoke of them as "manageable abstractions" (82-83). Paul Pennyfeather is not a hero but, says Waugh, a shadow of himself in most of *Decline and*

Fall; Adam Fenwick-Symes in *Vile Bodies* looks "exactly as young men like him do look" and speaks, on one occasion, "in no particular manner" (15, 33). Almost as obvious is Waugh's tendency to portray character by use of stereotype and caricature; in theory, and certainly in Waugh's practice, caricature involves the reduction of personality to near-abstraction, then presentation by means of a few qualifying characteristics that give the figure the only individuality it has. Accidents are as important as, in fact become, substance. Consciously or not, Waugh filled his early novels, especially the first three, with people who rush about in search of characteristics with which they can construct identity: questionnaire and interrogation, in which the external marks of individuality and motive are recorded, recur again and again in *Decline and Fall;* smart people and places and fashions, including green bowlers and suede evening shoes, are eagerly grasped at by the characters of *Vile Bodies;* in *Black Mischief,* the Emperor Seth seeks to define himself by frantically eclectic rummaging through catalogues of objects and compendiums of ideas.

Waugh's style also bears some marks of the classifier's attitude. Unlike Hemingway, for whom nouns and verbs, things and actions, are of primary importance, Waugh achieved some of his most telling effects by using striking adjectives and adverbs to modify relatively abstract terms. The roster of the Bollinger Club in *Decline and Fall* is one example: "epileptic royalty from their villas of exile; uncouth peers from crumbling country seats; smooth young men of uncertain tastes from the embassies and legations; illiterate lairds from wet granite hovels in the Highlands; ambitious young barristers and Conservative candidates torn from the London season and the indelicate advances of debutantes" (13-14). Here the adjectives establish the tone of humorous detachment; but on occasion Waugh used the same pattern to attack by frontal assault or to ambush with concealed pitfalls. His own early travel books, he wrote in *When the Going Was Good,* "were pedestrian, day-to-day accounts of things seen and people met, interspersed with commonplace information and some rather callow comments." More subtle and easier to pass over casually is the effect of adjectives like the one in Gilbert Pinfold's comparative estimate of his own books: "He thought them well made, better than many reputed works of genius" (4). The effect of "reputed" is delayed, so that the reader is jolted into an awareness that Pinfold is by no means mad with vanity. Here Waugh makes clear his separate classification of items that seem similar, a device shown even more clearly in his dismissal in *Ninety-Two Days* of anthropologists "flushed with the agnosticism of the provincial universities" (198).

In these last quotations, we are moving from caricature to discrimination. The former is primarily a matter of perception, a way of seeing the world in physical outline. The latter performs something of the same function in the moral sphere; it recognizes more than one possibility, but at some point—sooner in the mind of the satirist, later in that of the more subtle moralist—the various possibilities are stripped of complexity, measured, and judged. Waugh had from the beginning of his career a sense of what was important and what was not: a provincial university is not important; neither, really is "a world that has been well travelled by psychologists and satirists—the world of wild aberration without theological significance" (*Knox,* 314). This sense of discrimination accounted not only for his more intransigent political and religious stands but also for his tolerance, as a novelist and as a traveler, toward behavior that was odd, aberrant, and even disgusting, a tolerance that disturbed such diverse people as Cyril Connolly and the editor of the English Catholic newspaper, *The Tablet.* At twenty-five, Waugh delighted in observing the life of jolly brothels in Port Said; at fifty-five, he regarded with great interest the Star Bar in Mombasa, "a notorious dancing-bar, part brothel, part thieves' kitchen; everyone spoke of it with awe. . . . All races and all vices were catered for. I have never been in a tougher or more lively joint anywhere" (*Tourist in Africa,* 47). In his fiction, he could view without apparent shock or disapproval the depredations of Basil Seal or the German girl Kätchen; the passions of Captain Grimes, Ambrose Silk, and Anthony Blanche; and the callousness of Mrs. Beaver and Mr. Youkoumian. Yet his tolerance has essentially the same root as his lack of empathy. He once wrote, "as happier men watch birds, I watch men. They are less attractive but more various" (*Tourist in Africa,* 12), and his attitude toward them and toward everyone outside his sympathies was essentially that of an observer toward a specimen. He need not condemn them because they are outside the law and not liable to judgment. Of course, since they are not fully human, they get no more sympathy for being sheep than they would for being wolves: Mr. Joyboy is rightfully exploited by Dennis Barlow; the fat and stupid members of the upper middle classes are the natural prey of Basil Seal. In *They Were Still Dancing,* Waugh gave a theoretical basis for his objectivity: "It seems to me that a prig is someone who judges people by his own standards; criticism only becomes useful when it can show people where their own principles are in conflict" (61).

Waugh could not maintain this attitude. It was not perversity that drove him to abandon his position as detached, ironic observer—one quite congenial to him—for that of overt moralist and judge. The pressure of events after 1935—for Waugh the advent of a grim new age—drove him first to a conservatism which could advocate and celebrate Fascist victory in *Waugh in Abyssinia,* then to extol the glories of what he thought a vanishing class in *Brideshead Revisited,* and then to express loathing for, indeed resentment of, the postwar world in a manner that was only partly facetious. Beset with vexations and, like Rossetti, with an insomnia that could be alleviated only by drugs, he was assaulted by imaginary voices "in terms of 'gross and unbearable obloquy'" (*Rossetti,* 179). Unlike Rossetti, he did not attempt suicide, but silenced his voices and went on to produce four more books, one of which, *Unconditional Surrender* (in this country titled *The End of the Battle*), went beyond distinctions of class, race, and religion to exhibit sympathy and concern for impoverished Yugoslavian Jews.

Both the subject and sentiments of *Sword of Honour*, especially of *Unconditional Surrender*, did something to mollify critical opinion that had been exacerbated by the political stand of *Waugh in Abyssinia* and *Robbery Under Law* (in America, *Mexico: An Object Lesson*) and the social and religious attitudes expressed in *Brideshead Revisited*. Pointing to the obvious length and fundamental seriousness of the war trilogy as well as its positive moral views, critics like Bergonzi and Carens have seen it as the crowning achievement of Waugh's later career.

Throughout his career, however, Waugh's vision, as differentiated from his opinions, was essentially exclusive, defensive, reclusive. In positive terms, he advocated local loyalties and ties of custom rather than of rule, but it was chiefly in personal and negative terms that the vision found expression, so that the real theme of much of his work is "Save yourself; others you cannot save." Paul Pennyfeather retreated into theology, William Boot to the shabby comforts and the decaying certainties of Boot Magna, Dennis Barlow to England and the practice of his art, Scott-King to his boys' school and the classics, Guy Crouchback to the "Lesser House" and the placid domestic charms of the safe, conventional, agriculturally inclined Domenica Plessington. By his own account, Waugh shared this desire to escape, to burrow into the rock, "to create little private systems of order of his own" ("Fan-Fare," 60); in *A Little Learning* he linked to "the common English confusion of the antiquated with the sublime" his own tendency to seek "dark and musty seclusions, like an animal preparing to whelp" (44). It would be too simple to say that this reaction to experience makes Waugh an escapist, a romantic, or a reactionary. Certainly these were dangerous possibilities that sometimes became actualities, for instinctive condemnation and rejection of unpleasantness, if followed to a logical conclusion, leads either to fantasies of wish-fulfillment or shrill denunciation. However, while Waugh reacted to and rejected the chaos that he saw in modern life, he did not descend entirely into fantasy, and at his best he could perceive the inadequacy of the refuge as well as that of the world outside it.

III

The chief danger for such a writer is oversimplification, both morally and, at least for Waugh, technically, for just as his chief means of creating character was caricature, so his most common and most successful narrative or expository division was three or four pages, and even in his most consciously complex work he could seldom exceed either of these limits. To attain any degree of real complexity, whether of insight or narrative, he was forced to multiply, to develop concurrently several points of view and narrative strands. Whenever he did not do so, his work was weakest.

Waugh's need for technical and emotional complexity is seen most clearly in his short stories. Largely the product of the early 1930's, apparently written to keep the pot boiling, they are of very moderate quality indeed, particularly for a writer of Waugh's stature. Most of them depend for their effect upon the manipulation, through surprising turns of plot, of characters less wooden than cardboard. Neither character nor situation is much developed; Waugh himself seemed bored by conceptions that must have looked promising but had not worn very well.

The characters in Waugh's novels do not differ markedly in type from those in the short stories, and the actions in which they are involved are if anything less complex than those in the shorter form. Yet, by superimposing a series of cardboard figures one over the other, Waugh creates something more than a pack of cards. In *Vile Bodies,* for example, Simon Balcairn, Agatha Runcible, the Malpractices, Archie Schwert, and the rest of the

Bright Young People are by themselves trivial; put together in action and going each to his depressing end, they give an impression of a generation doomed, frustrated, and futile. An even clearer indication of Waugh's technique of reinforcement by repetition is his use of the double, ranging from the Boots in *Scoop* to Guy Crouchback's three counterparts in *Sword of Honour*. Throughout his career, Waugh used these devices, extensive rather than intensive, to construct his novels; such technical innovations as he introduced were designed not only to serve this end but to render less obvious, by interweaving as closely as possible the various characters and motifs, the fact that his basic method was so simple. *Decline and Fall*, perfect in its way, is in this respect comparatively crude, introducing and establishing characters chiefly by a series of monologues and then developing and resolving the plot-strands in discrete blocks, as indicated by chapter titles such as "Captain Grimes," "The Agony of Captain Grimes," and "The Passing of a Public School Man." *Vile Bodies*, though a lesser novel, is technically more advanced; Agatha Runcible's delirium, for example, draws together more vividly and effectively than had Professor Silenus' lecture in *Decline and Fall* the central themes and characters of the novel in the metaphor of the endless and meaningless race that is Waugh's objective correlative for the world without theological significance. In *A Handful of Dust*, Waugh brought to full maturity the techniques by which he achieved multiplicity and simultaneity; Tony's delirium, inhabited by the people and formed by the ideas that have betrayed him, is dramatic rather than merely rhetorical, and represents as great an advance over Agatha's rambling as that in its turn had over Silenus' discursive moralizing. The critics who, Waugh wrote in the "Preface" to the novel, "date my decline" from *A Handful of Dust* (7) were perhaps correct in a technical sense; there was nothing really new in his subsequent novels except the experiments with first-person narration in *Work Suspended* and *Brideshead Revisited*.

Judging from the narrator's comments in *Work Suspended,* Waugh was conscious that he was making a major change in this novel. Although the outbreak of World War II drove Waugh to abandon his theme and take up the new subject of war in something like his old form, he returned to first-person narrative in *Brideshead* before abandoning it altogether in his fiction. Waugh did not explain either the adoption or abandonment of this device, but his motives are not altogether enigmatic. John Plant told his publisher, "It seems to me I am in danger of becoming mechanical, turning out year after year the kind of book I know I can write well" (167). Furthermore, Waugh had begun to take a serious interest in religious and political questions. He may have felt that the first-person narrator would enable him to present in his fiction an attitude toward experience more searching, complex, and mature than that exhibited in the earlier novels; he may also have seen in this point of view a way of attaining a greater unity of effect.

Whatever his reasons, the experiments cannot be considered really successful either in technique or in maturity of point of view. Even Waugh was not satisfied; *Work Suspended* was revised in 1949 to cut extraneous material as well as shape the fragment for independent publication, and he altered the text of *Brideshead* at least twice before the acknowledged revision of 1960. As his excisions show, the first-person narrator whose experience, tastes, and attitudes to some extent paralleled his own had tempted him to introduce blocks of analysis, little essays several paragraphs long, that slow the pace and blur the focus. Even more important, the point of view became less complex than in the best of the early novels. Charles Ryder, the narrator of *Brideshead*, is by his own admission a dogmatic, even truculent defender of one philosophy after another—arcadian, agnostic-secularist, romantic, Christian. While he holds each view, he is impervious to criticism of it, though he can indulge in retrospective irony. Of course, Waugh intended his readers to accept the fourth

as the final and only impregnable position, but he gives
them even less evidence of its validity than he does of the
first three. Moreover, the technique could not guard
Waugh against going beyond the bounds of his basic
vision. Attacking rather than retreating from the world,
he seemed querulous and strident because he presented
his opinions overtly and without qualification.

IV

The basis of judgment for Waugh's novels, then, must
be the adequacy with which the vision is embodied: without balance and ironic contrast, Waugh could not develop
his central subject, the individual in retreat from a chaotic
and menacing society, into novels worthy of serious consideration; given proper form, the subject could sustain
novels that deserve to be read and remembered by pos-
terity. In these terms, *Vile Bodies, The Loved One,* and
Sword of Honour are of the second rank; *Scoop* and *Put
Out More Flags* are qualified successes; and *Decline and
Fall, Black Mischief,* and *A Handful of Dust* represent
Waugh's art and vision at their most effective.

The estimate of the first three novels listed may seem
surprising; though they have not been uniformly acclaimed
by his readers and critics, they have been regarded with
general respect. In none of them, however, is Waugh's recurring subject rendered adequately, with the result that
they are sentimental in the sense that facts are not pro-
portionate to the emotional response demanded. *Vile Bodies* provides the clearest example: the outer world is clearly established as mad and confusing by the events of the
novel, but the contrasting place of peace and security
sought by Adam and Nina is adumbrated only in the
Christmas scene at Doubting Hall (during an adulterous
love affair that is not judged in Christian terms). Throughout most of the book Waugh must depend upon direct
statement in his own voice or in that of his characters to
indicate to the reader the principles according to which

the action is to be judged. Consequently, the theme is too blatantly emphasized, while the narrative line, without effective contrast or thickening, is not very convincing.

The case of *The Loved One* is similar but more complex. Waugh is successful in showing the soulless, automatic responses of the people and the disorder of the society of Hollywood and Whispering Glades, inviting and easy targets for the satirist. But the novel lacks a moral center, a clear basis of judgment. Some critics have assumed that Waugh is contrasting Dr. Kenworthy's religion of death with the Christian view of death, judgment, heaven, and hell, an assumption that seems to be supported by Waugh's essay, "Death in Hollywood," on the art and values of Forest Lawn, which explicitly and forcefully makes this contrast. In the novel itself, however, no such basis for judgment or moral distinction exists. Neither Aimee's suicide nor Dennis's blackmail are condemned; both are the result of promptings of the spirit, remote, austere, amoral, and rather vague. Waugh seems to imply that the possession of any spirit whatever distinguishes these characters and Sir Francis Hinsley from the animals, two- and four-legged, that surround them. Even this standard is not consistently applied, however; Dennis's use of Aimee's death to effect his own withdrawal to England and the demands of his muse may be carried out ironically, but the basis of his superiority to Mr. Joyboy and Sir Ambrose Abercrombie has been undermined. If, on the other hand, he is acting under the compulsion of inspiration, of an inner necessity to write work of lasting value, then the dimensions and atmosphere of this refuge from the chaotic world need a more convincing presentation.

In its scope and its moral insights, *Sword of Honour* both intends to be and is a more considerable work than either *Vile Bodies* or *The Loved One*. Like Tennyson's *Idylls of the King*, it is impressive for its goal and method when considered in retrospect. The movement of the main story involves the related processes of stripping away Guy

Crouchback's illusions about the institutions of country, regiment, and class; of building in him a sense of his contact with humanity; and of breaking his spiritual paralysis. To illustrate and point up these processes, Waugh uses a series of comic scapegoats or doubles to dispel Guy's illusions by embodying them: Apthorpe as old soldier, Ivor Claire as detached aristocrat, and Ludovic as thrall, at least in his novel *The Death Wish,* to the idea of the type of woman who symbolizes the amoral grace and beauty of the 1920's. Yet, however well it employs this and a number of other devices, *Sword of Honour* is not fully satisfying as a work of art. It may be that the theme and the scope were too large for Waugh to render. Certainly he found it necessary to summarize, explain, and comment more frequently than in earlier novels, and many of these passages make the reading of the novel more tedious than the recollection of it. The book's length may also have made Waugh conscious of demands upon the reader's memory, so that he felt obliged to make quite explicit the comparisons and analogies, the motifs, and the recurrent bits of minor action that might have been more effective if better concealed.

The major weakness of the book is not narrowly technical, though it could be described as formal; it stems from the lack of alternatives and qualifications which marked *Vile Bodies* and *The Loved One.* Here it is detectable in the difference between the kinds of irony directed at Guy Crouchback and other members of the old order who are finally accepted, though they are misguided, and that which is aimed at almost all left-wingers and Americans, who are immediately rejected. The former is understanding if not indulgent: Guy behaves priggishly and stupidly, but his motives are logical and he is capable of moral change. The latter is scathing, expressed in names like Scab Dunz and Bum Schlum for the American journalists and Spitz (in the new edition Speit) for the American general, and judgment is simply pronounced rather than presented. But Waugh's political views and anti-American bias are themselves effects of a deeper attitude: a dislike not only of the modern world but of any successful institution. In *Helena,* designating Constantine a symbol of "Power without Grace," he was as censorious of the Emperor as he ever was of a modern politician. The difficulty both in *Helena* and *Sword of Honour* is that Waugh seemed unable to conceive of or at any rate to present in fiction the possibility of power with grace, and therefore chooses, not quite critically enough, grace without power, institutional forms, as represented by old Mr. Crouchback, without any real content, emphasizing the lack of power and making it almost a guarantee of grace. Waugh might not have agreed with Guy that only a fully just cause is worth pursuing, but he does not show clearly, as he did in some novels, the consequences of such an attitude.

Scoop and *Put Out More Flags* are more successful— not necessarily better—books than *The Loved One, Vile Bodies,* and *Sword of Honour* because they are less ambitious and because their form balances more perfectly the opposing forces in Waugh's vision. In *Scoop,* Boot Magna is William's refuge from the world of Lord Copper; in *Put Out More Flags,* the desire of Ambrose Silk and Cedric Lyne to remain individuals and aesthetes in a world that is organizing itself for war contrasts to the eagerness with which most of the characters—even, finally, Basil Seal—rush to join one herd or another. The books are less ambitious because the threats to security —journalism and the German war machine—are not shown as really serious. William escapes Lord Copper's publicity-mill by simple stubbornness; and although the Germans kill Cedric Lyne and the British drive Ambrose into exile, *Put Out More Flags* closes with a sense of release and triumph. Yet these books have a symmetry of form because both the world and the refuge are developed, so that one continually poses a criticism of the other. William Boot has escaped from the world's confusion,

detail, Tony's place of refuge is insubstantial and without real foundation, based on empty picturesqueness rather than a solid tradition. One may go further and say that Waugh is rejecting the aesthetic, the traditional, and the institutional approaches to life, for all are forms without content. The world of the novel is hollow. There is no content, though Waugh spares a minimal sympathy for those who embrace some sort of form. Yet both Tony's delusions and the callousness and aimlessness of the Londoners are exposed rather than condemned; both are the result of processes that the individual cannot control or even understand. In a sense, the innocent and the guilty are equally responsible and equally blameless. The novel presents a picture of how things are rather than a moral statement about them.

Ultimately, questions about the value of Waugh's work can be reduced to one crucial question of whether or not he gives in his art a vision not of the truth but of a truth. It seems quite clear that he does. His novels embody a series of variations on one central theme: the individual, to be saved as an individual, must retreat from modern society; institutions are finally not worthy of loyalty, though ideals and people are; power in the world inevitably corrupts, but renunciation of the world and of power involves a real cost; the pressure of events is toward greater confusion, increasing drabness, and vitiation of energy; and private salvation cannot be shared. These views may be partial, but they are neither irresponsible nor foolish, and at his best Waugh presents them in coherent and compelling fashion in novels of enduring value.

NOTES

1 References to Waugh's works will be given parenthetically in the text. What may be called the new uniform edition of Waugh's novels, published by Chapman and Hall with prefaces and alterations in the text by the author, represents his final intention. In this edition are *Decline and Fall, Vile Bodies, Black Mischief, A Handful of Dust, Scoop, Put Out*

More Flags, Brideshead Revisited, The Loved One, and *Sword of Honour* (the single-volume recension of *Men at Arms, Officers and Gentlemen,* and *Unconditional Surrender*). Cited from the first uniform edition (London, 1948-50) are *Helena, Scott-King's Modern Europe,* and *Work Suspended and Other Stories Written Before the Second World War.* Other editions cited: *The Ordeal of Gilbert Pinfold* (Boston, 1957); the travel books *When the Going Was Good* (Boston, 1947), *A Bachelor Abroad* (New York, 1930), *They Were Still Dancing* (New York, 1932), *Ninety-Two Days* (New York, 1934), *Waugh in Abyssinia* (New York, 1936), *Mexico: An Object Lesson* (Boston, 1939), and *Tourist in Africa* (Boston, 1960); and the biographies *Rossetti: His Life and Work* (London, 1928), *Monsignor Ronald Knox* (Boston, 1959), and *A Little Learning* (Boston, 1964). Interviews and essays cited are "Fan-Fare," *Life,* XX (April 8, 1946), 53-60; "Death in Hollywood," *Life,* XXII (September 29, 1947), 73-84; "An Open Letter . . . on a Very Serious Subject," *Noblesse Oblige,* ed. Nancy Mitford (London, 1956), pp. 65-82; Julian Jebb, "The Art of Fiction XXX: Evelyn Waugh," *Paris Review,* No. 30 (Summer-Fall, 1963), 72-85.

2 Some of these problems are outlined in my note, "Textual Problems in the Novels of Evelyn Waugh," in *Papers of the Bibliographical Society of America,* LXII (Second Quarter, 1968), 259-263. Anthony Newnham is at work on what promises to be a definitive bibliography; Jackson R. Bryer is compiling a check list of criticism.

BIBLIOGRAPHY

A Selected Check List

Bibliographies

Doyle, Paul A. "Evelyn Waugh: A Bibliography (1926-1956)," *Bulletin of Bibliography*, XXII (May-August, 1957), 57-62.

Kosok, Heinz. "Evelyn Waugh: A Checklist of Criticism," *Twentieth Century Literature*, XI (January, 1966), 211-215.

——————. "Evelyn Waugh: A Supplementary Checklist of Criticism," *Evelyn Waugh Newsletter*, II (Spring, 1968), 1-3.

Linck, Charles E., Jr. "Works of Evelyn Waugh, 1910 to 1930," *Twentieth Century Literature*, X (April, 1964), 19-25. (Linck's dissertation, "The Development of Evelyn Waugh's Career: 1903-1939" University of Kansas, 1963, carries the listing to 1939.)

Evelyn Waugh Newsletter, edited by Paul A. Doyle, carries current bibliographies, textual notes, and criticisms of Waugh's work.

Criticism

Bradbury, Malcolm. *Evelyn Waugh.* Edinburgh: Oliver and Boyd, 1964.

Carens, James F. *The Satiric Art of Evelyn Waugh.* Seattle, Wash.: University of Washington Press, 1966.

Cosman, Max. "The Nature and Work of Evelyn Waugh," *Colorado Quarterly,* IV (1956), 428-441.

Davis, Robert Murray. "Evelyn Waugh's Early Work: The Formation of a Method," *Texas Studies in Literature and Language,* VII (Spring, 1965), 97-108.

——————. "Evelyn Waugh on the Art of Fiction," *Papers on Language and Literature,* II (Summer, 1966), 243-252.

Dennis, Nigel. "Evelyn Waugh: The Pillar of Anchorage House," *Partisan Review,* X (July-August, 1943), 350-361.

Green, Peter. "Du Côté de Chez Waugh," *Review of English Literature,* II (April, 1961), 89-100.

Hall, James. "Stylized Rebellion: Evelyn Waugh," *The Tragic Comedians: Some Modern British Novelists.* Bloomington, Indiana: Indiana University Press, 1963.

Hardy, John Edward. *"Brideshead Revisited*: God, Man and Others," *Man in the Modern Novel.* Seattle: University of Washington Press, 1964.

Jebb, Julian. "The Art of Fiction XXX: Evelyn Waugh," *Paris Review,* No. 30 (Summer-Fall, 1963), 72-85.

Hines, Leo. "Waugh and His Critics," *Commonweal,* LXXVI (1962), 60-63.

Macaulay, Rose. "Evelyn Waugh," *Horizon,* XIV (December, 1946), 360-376.

Marcus, Steven. "Evelyn Waugh and the Art of Entertainment," *Partisan Review,* XXIII (Summer, 1956), 348-357.

Savage, D. S. "The Innocence of Evelyn Waugh," *Western Review,* XIV (Spring, 1950), 197-206.

Stopp, Frederick J. *Evelyn Waugh*: *Portrait of an Artist.* Boston: Little, Brown and Co., 1958.

Wasson, Richard. *"A Handful of Dust*: Critique of Victorianism," *Modern Fiction Studies,* VII (Winter, 1961-62), 327-337.

Wilson, Edmund. "'Never Apologize, Never Explain:' The Art of Evelyn Waugh" and "Splendors and Miseries of Evelyn Waugh," *Classics and Commercials.* New York: Farrar, Straus, 1950.

Wagon, Richard. A Paradigm of ... ...
... ... Western Person, London, ... Trigger
... ...

Wilson, Edmund. ... ... Henry ... ...
The Art of Henry Wandl ... and ... and ...
... ... of Edmund Wilson. Chicago ... ...
New York: Farrar Straus, 1956.

CONTRIBUTORS

ROBERT MURRAY DAVIS, B.S., Rockhurst College, M.A., University of Kansas, Ph.D., University of Wisconsin; has taught at Loyola University (Chicago), University of California, Santa Barbara, now assistant professor of English at the University of Oklahoma; has contributed articles on modern fiction and fictional theory to a number of scholarly journals and has lectured on fictional theory to scholarly organizations; editor, *The Novel: Modern Essays in Criticism,* currently completing a study of the novels of Ronald Firbank.

ALVIN B. KERNAN, Professor of English, Yale University, has published widely on satire and satirists in all genres; among his major works are *The Cankered Muse* and *The Plot of Satire* and a collection, *Modern Satire.*

CHARLES E. LINCK, JR., A.B. (*Magna cum Laude*), Saint Benedict's College, M.S., Kansas State University, Ph.D., University of Kansas; associate professor of English, East Texas State University; associate editor of *Evelyn Waugh Newsletter;* articles on Waugh in *Twentieth Century Literature* and *Papers on Language and Literature.*

PATRICIA CORR received her B.A. and M.A. (honors) at the National University of Ireland, University College, Dublin; Senior English Teacher, Sion Hill College, Dublin; has published articles on criticism and methodology, *Modern Novelists—A Catholic Approach,* and a text book, *The Anthology of Short Stories;* currently preparing a book on the English classical novel.

D. J. DOOLEY, B.A., University of Western Ontario, M.A., University of Toronto, Ph.D., State University of Iowa;

professor of English, Saint Michael's College, University of Toronto; has published essays on satire and on the novel in various scholarly journals, *The Art of Sinclair Lewis,* and articles on political and religious subjects.

MARSTON LAFRANCE, B.A., Harpur College, M.A., Cornell, Ph.D., University of Wisconsin; Associate Professor of English, Carleton University, Ottawa, Canada; has published articles and reviews in scholarly journals and has edited *Patterns of Commitment in American Literature;* currently at work on a book-length study of Stephen Crane.

BERNARD BERGONZI, M.A. and B.Litt., Oxford University; senior lecturer in English, University of Warwick, and has taught at Manchester University and Brandeis University; has written *The Early H. G. Wells*: *A Study of the Scientific Romances* and *Heroes' Twilight*: *A Study of the Literature of the Great War* and later this year will publish *The Situation of the Novel;* has edited H. G. Well's *Tono-Bungay,* George Gissing's *New Grub Street,* and *Innovations*: *Essays on Art and Ideas.*

116